MELODY WRITING AND ANALYSIS

By the same author

A GRADED MUSIC COURSE FOR SCHOOLS
Book One
Book Two
Book Three

SCORE READING, FORM AND HISTORY
Book Four of *A Graded Music Course for Schools*

ADDITIONAL SIGHTSINGING EXERCISES
For use with *A Graded Music Course for Schools*

HARMONY

READ, SING AND PLAY
Pupils' Book One
Pupils' Book Two
Teacher's Book One
Teacher's Book Two

ANALYSES OF MUSICAL CLASSICS
Book One
Book Three

BASIC MUSIC KNOWLEDGE

GRADED AURAL TESTS FOR ALL PURPOSES

MELODY WRITING AND ANALYSIS

by

Annie O. WARBURTON
Mus. D., L.R.A.M., A.R.C.M.

LONGMAN

LONGMAN GROUP LIMITED
London

*Associated companies, branches and representatives
throughout the world*

Second edition © Annie O. Warburton 1960

*First published 1952
New impressions 1953; 1955; 1956; 1959
Second edition 1960
New impressions 1962; 1963; 1965;
1968; 1969; 1970*

ISBN 0 582 32591 9

*Printed in Hong Kong by
Dai Nippon Printing Co (International) Ltd*

PREFACE

This book is intended as a companion to 'Harmony' and tries to do for melody writing and analysis what that book aimed at doing for harmony.

Music Educationists all agree on the value of melody writing, and most Examining Bodies require it, yet there seems to have been little attempt at supplying a complete and carefully graded text book on the subject. The art of melody writing can, however, be divided into easy stages and studied systematically, to the great musical benefit of the student.

The experience of correcting some thousands of music papers set in various public examinations has shown the writer how many students, some of them really musical, have no idea how to set to work to compose or to analyse a melody. They lack guidance and this book sets out to help them. Its method and technique are the outcome of many years of experience and the course has already been tried out by a number of colleagues in the schools.

Parts I and II cover the ground required for tune writing at the Ordinary Level of the General Certificate of Education ; reference to Part III and a study of Part V prepare for melody analysis questions in the same examination ; while Part VI gives practice in analysis of an unprepared piece of piano music, which is also required by some of the Examining Boards. Therefore the book, together with 'Harmony for Schools and Colleges,' covers all the ground required for this examination except for the study of set works, which varies from year to year.

Parts III and IV will be found of use at the Advanced Level of the General Certificate of Education and the book as a whole should serve the needs of candidates working for the higher theory examinations of the Associated Board of the Royal Schools of Music, for examinations in Training Colleges and Colleges of Music and for music diplomas.

But the book is not intended merely to be an examination text-book. There are many musical students who wish they could compose melodies, and this book should give them the stimulus and help they need.

Part I deals with the elementary stages of melody writing. The work is carefully graded, each new point of construction, each new technical or notational difficulty being dealt with separately. Tunes in simple time are written before those in compound time ; tunes in major keys before those in minor keys ; two bar phrases before four bar phrases ; masculine endings before feminine endings, etc.

Anacrusic rhythms and the subdivision of the phrase are dealt with early, as they are so essential ; and the use of development is illustrated as soon as the student is ready to deal with eight bar melodies.

Irregular phrasing is not introduced in this section, and the writer feels strongly that it should not be attempted until the student has developed a good rhythmic sense.

Part I goes as far as the composition of regular sixteen bar melodies with a modulation to the dominant or relative major, and it will, therefore, fulfil the requirements of the General Certificate of Education at the Ordinary Level.

Part II applies all that has been learnt in Part I to the composition of melodies to words. It is the writer's experience that students can best conquer the various difficulties which arise in tune writing if they concentrate on the tune alone at first, without having to learn about the treatment of words at the same time. Words are a stimulus to young children in the earliest stages, particularly if the tune is improvised rather than written down, but difficulties arise as soon as anything more than simple doggerel is set. In addition to knowing the notational rules, the student must be able to divide words into syllables, have an understanding of accent and metre and a good rhythmic sense. His rhythmic feeling will make him often wish to set the words in $\frac{6}{8}$ time and he must, therefore, be thoroughly familiar with compound time notation.

Accordingly the writer recommends that Part I should be finished before Part II is begun. But it is possible to study

Sections 1-7 of Part II after Sections 1-5 of Part I have been done, if compound time is known. Sections 6-8 of Part I must have been studied before four line verses are attempted and there are other places where the knowledge gained in Part I is applied to Part II.

Part II goes as far as the setting of four line stanzas, using all kinds of metrical feet, to which regular two or four bar phrases can easily be set.

Part III continues melodic composition to the stages required for the Advanced Level of the General Certificate of Education and the various music diplomas. It includes irregular phrasing and longer pieces in binary and ternary form with modulations to all the related keys, and it suggests that the student should either indicate the keys and cadence chords or write simple accompaniments to the tunes.

Part IV applies Part III to the setting of poetry and includes examples of longer and more irregular stanzas.

Part V deals with Melody Analysis. The student who has worked through Parts I and III and who has therefore been analysing all the time, will find this section easy, and will require little more than plenty of exercises on which to practise. Some teachers may, however, wish to start Part V as soon as Part I is finished. It is not necessary to have composed irregular phrases oneself, or to have modulated to a number of related keys before recognising these devices in the work of others. It is possible therefore to read through Part III without actually working the exercises, and then to proceed immediately to the analysis in Part V.

Unprepared analysis of a simple piano piece, such as is required by some Examining Bodies, grows naturally out of a study of the preceding sections ; but Part VI gives further guidance and some exercises to work, as it is difficult to provide sufficient copies of a piece of music for a whole class.

The book is copiously illustrated with examples and includes a large number of exercises.

PREFACE TO THE SECOND EDITION

The second edition includes an appendix on writing accompaniment to melodies, which should be helpful to "A" Level pupils whose Examining Boards require them to harmonise their melodies or to sketch in a bass.

CONTENTS

PART I.
ELEMENTARY MELODY WRITING.

PART II.
THE SETTING OF WORDS TO A MELODY: REGULAR, SHORT STANZAS.

B

Part III.
More Advanced Melody Writing.

Part IV.
More Advanced Melody Writing to Words.

PART V.
MELODY ANALYSIS.

PART VI.
ANALYSIS OF SHORT PIANO PIECES.

PUBLISHER'S NOTE

Acknowledgments for permission to include copyright material are due to the following :—

Messrs. J. B. Cramer & Co., London, England, for excerpts from *The Dragon Fly*, melody by Martin Shaw, words by Mary Howitt, and from *Twilight Lullaby*, melody by T. Dunhill, words by Amy Dooley ; The Executors of Sir Walford Davies for part of the melody of *The Dirge* ; Messrs. Novello & Co. Ltd., for excerpts from the melodies of the following songs : *My Heart is Like a Singing Bird, From a City Window*, and *Armida's Garden*, by Hubert Parry, *Boats and Bridges* by May Sarson, *Charming Chloe* by Edward German, and *The Brook* by Eric H. Thiman.

PART I

ELEMENTARY MELODY WRITING

1 Preamble

Many musical people can sing, hum, or whistle an original tune quite easily—particularly if no one is listening ! But very few can remember and write down what they have so spontaneously composed. Because this is difficult some people are so unwise as to attempt to ' manufacture ' a tune, without hearing it in their heads first. This may *seem* easier, but it never results in a good tune ! More often than not it is ' musical nonsense ' ! Here are two tunes : (*a*) is musical sense ; (*b*) is musical nonsense.

Fig.1   Lullaby. Schubert

The only musical way to compose is to think in musical ideas, or phrases, however short, even though this is harder to write down than if you thought of a note or two at a time. When writing English you think in phrases, not in separate words, though you may spend some time later in polishing your thought and changing a word here and there. Exactly the same is true of music. The unit of thought is the phrase.

Therefore, when writing a melody, sing your musical idea aloud or in your head first, then memorise it, if you think it good, and finally write it down as if you were working a dictation exercise, using solfa and time names. This may seem a long way round but it will result in musical

sense. When you have written your tune check it to be
sure you have written what you meant, and *add the phrase
marks*. A tune without phrase marks is like a sentence
without punctuation.

In order to help you to write ' musical sense ' in your first
melodies the phrases will be short and simple enough for you
to hear in your head and remember, and the following
limitations will be temporarily imposed :—

(a) Exercises will be in ²₄ and ³₄ time, major keys only.

(b) Every phrase must be *exactly* two bars long.

(c) The last note of every phrase must occur on a strong
    beat.

(d) Tunes will consist of two phrases. The first phrase
    can end on any note except *doh* (*soh, te, ray* and *me* are
    the best) ; the second phrase must end on *doh*.

(e) Keep to stepwise movement as far as possible, and do
    not move by a larger interval than a third except
    between notes of the *doh* and *soh* chords.

These limitations will be removed one by one at later
stages, as your knowledge and ability grow.

2   The Two Bar Phrase—Question and Answer

A short two bar phrase is frequently balanced by another
two bar phrase, the two sounding rather like a question and
answer.

Exercise I. ' Answer ' the following ' Questions ', using
the rhythms given. End on *doh*. Be sure you have sung the
' Question' correctly (using sol-fa) before you make up your
' Answer '.

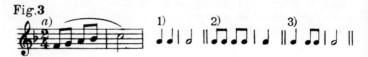

Exercise II. 'Answer' the following 'Questions', making up both rhythm and tune. Model your rhythms on those in Fig. 3. They must sound as if they belong to the first half, and the first and last notes must occur on the strong accent. End on *doh*. Give three 'Answers' to each 'Question'.

Fig.4

3   Anacrusic Rhythm

Phrases which begin on a weak beat are termed 'anacrusic'.

Fig. 5 shows an anacrusic question and answer.

Fig.5

Notice that the phrases are *exactly* two bars in length, as each begins on the third beat and ends on the second. This is usually the case, and you are advised to keep to this method at present, so that if you are given an anacrusic phrase you answer it by an anacrusic one, and vice versa.

Anacrusic phrasing gives a forward lilt to a tune (compare the *Marseillaise* with *God save the King*) and an anacrusic tune often comes into one's head more easily than one beginning on the strong beat, but more care is needed in writing it down. Be sure that the bar lines are in the right place, i.e., before the strong accents, not necessarily at the beginning of each phrase. It is a common fault to confuse phrasing with bar lines. Many people instinctively, but quite wrongly, put a bar line when they come to the end of a phrase, thus treating the bar line as if it were a punctuation mark. It is true that *double* bars are used to denote a phrase ending, especially in hymn tunes. But the single bar line has nothing to do with phrasing, and it is of great importance to realise this clearly before going on to more advanced stages.

In counting bars the first *complete* bar is called bar one, and we reckon the number of bars in a phrase by the number of first beats that the phrase contains.

Exercise III. ' Answer ' the following ' Questions ' using the rhythms given. End on *doh*.

Fig. 6

Exercise IV. ' Answer ' the following ' Questions ', making up both rhythm and tune. The rhythm must be anacrusic. The last note must occur on the strong beat and be held over to the length required to complete the two bar phrase. (See examples in Fig. 6.) Give three ' Answers ' to each ' Question '.

Fig. 7

Exercise V. 'Answer' the following 'Questions', giving two versions of each.

Fig.8

4 The Rhythmic Structure of the Four Bar Phrase

The most usual length of a phrase is four bars.

Fig.9

Golden Slumbers

Many four bar phrases divide into two sections and sometimes these sections sub-divide again into units consisting of a short rhythmic figure. A section is usually exactly two bars long and a unit exactly one bar, which means that, with an anacrusic rhythm, the divisions will *not* coincide with the bar lines and a two bar section may spread itself over parts of three different bars, as in Fig. 10(*a*).

Fig.10

The Marseillaise

Violin Concerto. Beethoven

It is very common for a phrase to be divided into two sections, and for the first section to be broken into units, while the second is continuous, as at Fig. 10(*b*). Compare this with Fig. 11, which is too broken up.

Fig.11

Exercise VI. Sing the following phrases, taking breaths where your instinct tells you there is a slight break. Then indicate these breaks by means of phrase marks.

Fig. 12

From these illustrations you will deduce the following : (1) A repeated rhythm tends to break up the phrase (see (*b*) above). (2) A repeated anacrusis tends to break up the phrase (see (*a*) and (*c*) above). Therefore if you wish a phrase rhythm to continue unbroken take care to keep on moving at points where the rhythm might tend to break. Compare the following phrases ; then change the phrasing round while keeping the rhythms the same, and you will find they do not work.

Fig. 13

Exercise VII. Given the following beginnings, write four bar phrase rhythms, and add any phrase marks required. Let your rhythms grow naturally out of the given beginnings, with a reasonable amount of variety. Give two versions of each as follows : (1) Divided into two sections ; (2) Divided into two units (using the same rhythm) and one section, as in Fig. 13 (b) and (c). It will be a help if you make a sort of skeleton plan with bar lines and phrase marks, before you invent the rhythm, thus :—

Fig. 14

5 Melodic Line

When a melodic part moves by step it is said to be 'conjunct'. When it moves by leap it is 'disjunct'. Good vocal tunes usually move by conjunct movement with occasional leaps. It is possible to write a good tune with hardly any leaps.

Fig. 15   We be three poor Mariners

Beware of too many repeated notes in a melody, they tend to make it 'stick'.

Leaps of sixths and sevenths should be sparingly used, as they are difficult to sing. Octaves are sometimes quite easy. Quickly moving notes should generally move by step.

The notes before and after a large leap should be within it. Sing Fig. 16 (a), (b) and (c). Even quite small leaps, if two or more are taken in the same direction, can sometimes be awkward. See (d). After stepwise movement it is usually wise to leap in the opposite direction. See (e).

Fig. 16

A good vocal melody is always singable. Instrumental melodies sometimes jump much more freely than vocal ones, because the performer has not to hear the note in his head before he produces it. But it is wise to learn to write vocal melodies first.

Te has a natural tendency to move to *doh*. It can move to another note of the chord V, however, as in Fig. 17 (*a*) or down the scale by step as in Fig. 17 (*b*). Do not move from *fah* up to *te* ; it is awkward to sing. See Fig. 17 (*c*). (You may have already learnt that *fah te* is the only augmented interval that occurs in a major key and that augmented intervals have to be avoided.) *Fah* may move down to *te* provided that the next note is *doh*. See Fig. 17 (*d*). (This is the only diminished interval in a major key and must resolve inwards.) If *te* rises to *fah*, then the next note should be *me*. See Fig. 17 (*e*).

Fig. 17

Do not let your tune meander aimlessly round the same notes. It must travel with a purpose and even a short tune is better for having a climax.

Exercise VIII. (a) Write a four bar phrase starting as at Fig. 18 (*a*) without a single leap. End on *doh*.

(b) Fill in the gaps at Fig. 18 (*b*) as directed.

(c) Write a suitable note at the places marked * in Fig. 18 (*c*).

(d) Write four bar phrases beginning as at Fig. 18 (*d*), (*e*), (*f*) and (*g*). Show any subdivisions by phrase marks. Give two versions of each, as in Exercise VII.

Fig. 18

6   Unity and Variety in the Eight Bar Sentence— Repetition

Two four bar phrases frequently answer each other to make an eight bar sentence. There must be unity of idea throughout the sentence, and this is frequently obtained by repetition. Much more repetition is needed in music than in poetry, in order to produce a satisfactory effect. There must be variety also, though very little is required in an eight bar sentence.

Compare Fig. 19 (*a*), (*b*) and (*c*). (*a*) has a suitable amount of unity and variety, as the two sections of the first phrase are contrasted, while the second phrase is almost identical with the first. (*b*) has too much unity, and (*c*) has too much variety.

Fig. 19   The Lorelei

Unity is frequently obtained by repeating a phrase or a section of a phrase. Study the following models :—

(1) *AA* with a twist at the end of the second A to bring it back to *doh*. Undivided phrases.

Fig. 20

(2) *ABAB* with a slight alteration at the end so as to end on *doh*.

Fig. 21

(3) *ABAC.*

Fig. **22**

Give me thy hand.   Mozart

Figs. 21 and 22 each consist of two phrases divided into sections. It is possible to think of them as consisting of four short phrases, however, and it does not matter very much which way you look at it, as the word 'phrase' is a very loose term. It is not necessary to end on the first beat of the bar in bars 2 and 6, though it is still advisable for you to do so in bars 4 and 8.

Exercise IX. Given the following beginnings, complete each tune on the model of Fig. 20.

Fig. **23**

Exercise X. Given the following beginnings complete each tune (1) on the model of Fig. 21 ; (2) on the model of Fig. 22.

Fig. **24**

Exercise XI.   Given the following beginnings, complete each tune (1) on the model of Fig. 21 ; (2) on the model of Fig. 22. Before you begin, make out a skeleton scheme as shown below in order to keep yourself 'on the rails'.

Fig. 25

7   Development

Sometimes an idea is developed instead of repeated. Study the following models :

(1) *A A^d A A^d.* A^d develops A by repeating the last half in units. It might have been at a different pitch, as at Fig. 26 (*b*).

Fig. 26

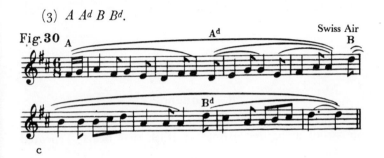

(2) *A A^d A B*. (a) A^d develops A by changing the interval of the first leap.

Fig. 27

Lavender's Blue

(b) A^d develops A ' by inversion '.

Fig. 28

Some folks do

(c) A^d develops A by repeating it at a different pitch. (It need not have been an exact reproduction.)

Fig. 29

Polly put the kettle on

(3) *A A^d B B^d*.

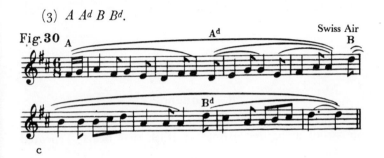

Fig. 30

Swiss Air

c

(4) *A B A^d C.*

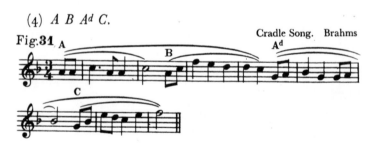

Fig.31

Cradle Song.   Brahms

N.B. C might perhaps be called B^d in this tune. Sometimes a phrase is on the border line in this way.

Exercise XII. Given the following beginnings, complete each tune on the models of Fig. 26-31 in turn. Follow the principle of the model rather than its detailed application. The development of a figure may prevent you from ending on the strong beat at bar 4. After you have written a tune on each model try to develop the idea in yet another way, on your own. (Some of these workings might be improvised in the lesson, rather than written out.)

Fig.32

8   Sequence

A special kind of development is 'Sequence'. This consists of a figure lasting at least two beats, repeated *immediately* at a higher or lower pitch. ' Polly put the kettle on ' and ' Swiss Air ', Figs. 29 and 30, contain examples of sequence. Study also the following models :—

One bar sequence at the beginning of the tune.

Bars 3 and 4 as sequences of bar 2.

Two bar sequence at the beginning of the tune.

One bar sequence at the beginning of the second half of the tune.

A sequence tends to become monotonous if repeated exactly more than once. If used a third time it is better varied or decorated, as at * in Fig. 36.

Some sequences sound best when repeated a second higher ; others may sound better a third higher, while yet others may be more effective a second or third lower, and so on. The reason is that one position implies satisfactory harmonic progressions while another one does not. If you accurately hear what you write your instinct will guide you in this matter. Nothing shows up weak aural ability more than unmusical sequences.

A sequence is often improved by being slightly varied or modified in some way. Again, harmonic considerations are often the reason for this.

Exercise XIII. Given the following beginnings, complete each tune on the model of Fig. 33.

Fig. 37

Exercise XIV. Given the following beginnings, complete each tune on the model of Figs. 34 to 36, in turn.

Fig. 38

9   The Silent Bar

In tunes with simple rhythms and only a few notes in a bar you will sometimes feel a desire to end at bar 7 instead of bar 8. But your rhythmic feeling should tell you that bar 8 is still required, either as a tied note or a rest. This extra bar is sometimes called ' the silent bar '.

Fig.39   Sweet Nightingale

Occasionally in folk tunes a three bar phrase will be found balancing four bar ones, as in Fig. 40, but most people will instinctively wait a 'silent' bar before beginning the next verse. Sing Fig. 40 to test this.

Fig.40   German Folk tune

Exercise XV. Complete the following beginnings to make eight bar tunes. Bar 8 is to consist of a tied note or a rest.

Fig.41

10 $\frac{4}{4}$ Time. Phrases Ending at the Half Bar

In $\frac{4}{4}$ time you will sometimes feel that the last note of the phrase wants to come *later* than you expect—on the third beat of the bar instead of the first. This is why $\frac{4}{4}$ time has not been introduced until now.

Fig.42   Outward and Homeward Bound

As the third beat in ⁴⁄⁴ time carries a fairly strong accent this is satisfactory. It happens more frequently at the end of subordinate phrases than at the end of main ones, but it depends upon the context, and your own rhythmic feeling must be your chief guide. Phrases can also end at the half bar in ²⁄₄, ⁶⁄₈ and ¹²⁄₈ time.

Two bar phrases are more common in ⁴⁄₄ than in ²⁄₄ or oɪ ³⁄₄ time, as there are probably more notes to the bar. The difference between Figs. 42 and 43 is slight, and sometimes you will find composers carelessly writing one way when they mean the other.

Fig. 43

Exercise XVI. Complete the following beginnings to make eight bar tunes. They can be built on any plan you like, as long as they have unity and regular rhythmic shape. But label each phrase.

Fig. 44

Exercise XVII. Write eight bar tunes on the following rhythms. Phrase the rhythms first.

Fig. 45

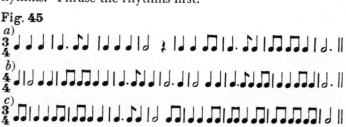

11 Implied Harmony

In Western Europe and America anyone hearing a tune nowadays unconsciously imagines a harmonic background. Play the tune in Fig. 46 (*a*). Then play (*b*) and (*c*).

Fig. 46

Even an unmusical person will feel that the harmonies at (*b*) fit, and his ear will be outraged by those at (*c*). If he had not possessed some preconceived notion on hearing (*a*), he would not have objected to (*c*). We and our ancestors have heard harmonic music for 300 years, and our instincts have been developed in this way. A primitive African would probably not feel one version any better than the other, because he has not our harmonic instincts.

A good tune can almost always be harmonised easily. If your teacher has sometimes improvised harmonies to your previous efforts you will have realised the truth of this, for there is no better way of testing a tune. It is a good plan to build tunes on harmonic schemes, though this limits you to harmonic progressions that you already know.

Example : ¾ I – – |IV – – |V – – |I – – || could be treated thus :—

Fig. 47

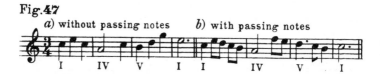

a) without passing notes   b) with passing notes

You have been warned to use large leaps sparingly. It is generally good, however, to leap from one chord note to another, particularly over I, IV and V. Fig. 48 is rather an extreme example.

Fig. 48   The Ash Grove

Exercise XVIII. Make up tunes on the following chord schemes. Each chord is to last for one bar. Do not jump too much.

(a) I IV I V ; I IV V I.

(b) I IV II V ; V VI IV I.

(c) I VI IV V ; VI II V I.

12   Cadences

The last few notes of a phrase make what is called a 'cadence'. The type of cadence takes its name from the final chords which are present or implied. The last two chords usually move from a weak to a strong accent.

THE PERFECT CADENCE. This consists of the chords of the dominant and tonic, V I. In the melody any note of V may move to any note of I, though in practice the melody generally moves smoothly. The 7th is frequently added to V .

Fig. 49

Fig. 50 shows three harmonised perfect cadences, and two melodies in which the perfect cadence is implied.

Fig. 50

a) God save the Queen

b)   Op. 14 No. 2. Beethoven

c)   Op. 7.   Beethoven

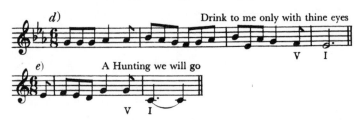

THE PLAGAL CADENCE. This consists of the subdominant chord followed by the tonic, IV I. It is as finished as the perfect cadence, though considerably less common.

Fig. 51

THE INTERRUPTED CADENCE. A cadence is said to be interrupted when V is the penultimate chord and the ear expects I, but some unexpected chord is put in its place. The unexpected chord is often VI, but it may be a chromatic discord. Compare the three versions of 'All through the Night' in Fig. 52

Fig. 52

THE IMPERFECT CADENCE. An imperfect cadence usually ends with V, and almost any chord may precede it. Imperfect cadences which do not end on V are occasionally found, and in practice, any cadence which is not finished and not interrupted may be called imperfect. I IV is frequently found.

Fig. 53

Op. 14, No. 2. Beethoven

a)

b) Auld Lang Syne

Exercise XIX. Following the example of Fig. 54 write three different melodic endings implying the following cadences. Insert the bar lines.

Perfect in G and B♭ major ; Plagal in F and A major ; Interrupted in D and E♭ major; Imperfect in C and E major. (Use any note but *te* before V.)

Fig. 54

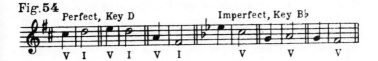

Perfect, Key D   Imperfect, Key B♭

Exercise XX. Working as shown below write four bar phrases beginning as follows. Use each beginning four times and end with a perfect, plagal, interrupted and imperfect cadence, in turn.

Fig.55

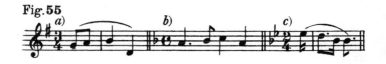

Work thus :—

(1) Copy the given beginning and mark the bar lines for the complete phrase.

(2) Write the names of the chords required at the cadence under the staff, taking care that the last chord comes on the strong accent.

(3) Write the letter names of the cadence notes available for the tune, above the staff. Your exercise will now look like this :—

Fig.56

(4) Fill in the rest of the phrase. The last two notes must be chosen from the names you have written above the staff, and they must move smoothly and naturally.

Exercise XXI. Working on similar lines to Ex. XX, write eight bar tunes beginning as in Fig. 57. Choose your own cadences. The cadence at bar 4 can be perfect, imperfect or plagal, but avoid *doh* for the final note. The cadence at bar 8 must be perfect or plagal. There is no point in using an interrupted cadence at present, as without the presence of harmonies, it cannot be distinguished from a perfect. Work each beginning three times.

13   Cadence Decoration

Melodies frequently decorate their cadence chords. Fig. 58 shows some decorations over an imperfect cadence.

In (*a*) and (*b*) the implied chords are still easily recognisable. To write or recognise (*c*) and (*d*) requires a more advanced knowledge.

Remember that the final cadence *chord* will normally occur on the last strong accent, even though the decorations continue. When the last *melody* note also occurs on the strong accent the end is said to be ' masculine '; when, because of decoration, it occurs on a weak beat the ending is ' feminine '.

It is particularly common for the melody to fall by step to the chord note as at Fig. 58 (*c*). Feminine endings are more common at the end of subordinate phrases than at the end of a section or piece.

Fig.59

Annie Laurie

Exercise XXII. Rewrite a few of the phrases you have written in previous tunes, decorating the cadences melodically. The simplest method is to put your last note a beat later, and write an extra note (quite possibly the note above) on the strong beat.

Exercise XXIII. Write phrases of your own leading to
    (a) an imperfect cadence, masculine ending ;
    (b) an imperfect cadence, feminine ending ;
    (c) a plagal cadence, masculine ending ;
    (d) a perfect cadence, feminine ending ;
    (e) a perfect cadence, masculine ending.

14   Compound Time

Writing in compound time often causes trouble, perhaps because people are not sufficiently sure of its notation.

In ⁶₈ time a good tune can be written, using only the time patterns ♩. , ♫♪ , ♩ ♪ and a long note at the ends of the phrases.

Fig. 60   London Bridge

If ♪.♫♩ is added to the above rhythmic figures sufficient rhythmic variety can be obtained for any simple tune.

Fig. 61   The Gentle Maiden

The effect of ¾ time and ⁶⁄₈ time is often almost identical.

Fig. 62   Lilliburlero

Waltzes are always written in ¾ time but in rhythmic effect two bars of a waltz make up one bar of ⁶⁄₄ time.

Sing ' The Blue Danube ' to yourself to test this.

Fig. 63 (*a*) shows a ⁶⁄₈ tune using other subdivisions of the beat and (*b*) and (*c*) show tunes in ⁹⁄₈ and ¹²⁄₈ time. Both the the latter times are rare.

Fig. 63

The Lament of Flora Macdonald

German Folk Song

Prelude 9 of "the 48". Bach

Exercise XXIV. Write eight bar tunes, beginning as follows. Use only ♩. , ♫♫ , ♩ ♪ and a long note at the end of each phrase. Label your phrases, or use a plan dictated by your teacher.

Fig. 64

N.B.—A tune quite often runs round a pivot note, as at (*d*).

Exercise XXV.   Write eight bar tunes beginning as follows. Then re-write them in ¾ time.

Fig. 65

Exercise XXVI.   Write eight bar tunes beginning as follows.

Fig. 66

15   The Minor Mode

The minor mode is full of pitfalls for the unwary ! If the harmonic form of the scale is used there are four augmented intervals to be avoided.

Fig. 67

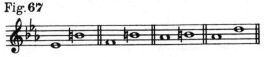

Their inversions are, of course, diminished, and they may be sparingly used if the next note is inside the leap. It is a good rule to approach the leading note from above, unless from the dominant, in order to avoid augmented intervals. Remember that the leading note requires an accidental.

The use of the melodic minor helps matters a little, but in order to keep the tonality clear it is advisable to approach and quit the sixth and seventh degrees of the scale by step.

D

Occasionally the ascending form may be used descending and vice versa. But your sole guide on this matter will have to be your ear. Do not use the flattened seventh at a cadence, unless you intend to write a tune in one of the old modes.

Fig. 68 shows two minor mode tunes, the second one using the melodic minor.

Exercise XXVII. Write eight bar tunes beginning as follows. Use the harmonic form of the minor scale only.

Exercise XXVIII. Write eight bar tunes beginning as follows. Use the melodic form of the minor scale at least once in each.

16 Twelve Bar Melodies

Study the following models.

Exercise XXIX. Write twelve bar tunes, beginning as follows. Give two versions of each. One version must be based on one of the above models, the other must be on a plan of your own.

Fig.75

17 Sixteen Bar Melodies

Study the following models. Notice that if a tune is to contain four phrases the first can end on *doh*. But the second phrase should rarely do so, unless it is a repetition of the first. The third phrase must never end on *doh*, as it is too near the end.

Notice the use of development within the phrase, as well as repetitions and developments of whole phrases.

Fig.76 A A B A   All through the Night

Fig.77 A A B A^d   The British Grenadiers

It is not essential to keep to the same style of rhythm throughout a tune (See Fig. 78 which changes to anacrusic rhythm at B.) But be sure that a change sounds satisfactory.

A tune of sixteen bars or longer will also gain by having
a climax in rhythm and pitch, or both. It normally occurs
in the second half of the tune. Sometimes it is produced by
using the quicker notes of the original time pattern more
continuously than at the beginning and working them up to
a high note. See Fig. 84.

Fig. 84

It may be caused by rising sequences or by a long note or
a pause.

Fig. 85

Breathe on me, breath of God

In Fig. 86 it is caused by the gradual reaching up to the
highest note, which only occurs once, towards the end.
Notice the beautiful curves in this example.

Fig. 86

The Londonderry Air

Most sixteen bar tunes contain at least one modulation, and you may find yourself wishing to modulate when you start to write your own. But it is possible to write good tunes of this length without doing so, as the examples given above show. You will be shown how to modulate in section 18. In the meantime keep to a fairly simple style with plenty of repetition and not too much subdivision of phrase, and you should then be able to keep to the one key.

Exercise XXX. Write sixteen bar tunes beginning as follows, using Figs. 76 to 83 as models in turn. (As this means writing forty tunes your teacher had better say which you are to do !)

Fig. 87

Exercise XXXI. Write original tunes as follows. First get a musical idea in your head, then write it down and afterwards build the rest of the tune up from this.

    (a) An eight bar tune in G major in $\frac{6}{8}$ time.
    (b) An eight bar tune in D minor in $\frac{3}{4}$ time.
    (c) A twelve bar tune in E major in $\frac{2}{4}$ time.
    (d) A sixteen bar tune in E minor in $\frac{6}{8}$ time.
    (e) A sixteen bar tune in F major in $\frac{3}{4}$ time.

18   Modulation to the Dominant

Modulation is one of the most useful means of getting variety into a tune. By now you will be wishing to modulate and will have realised the need for using this device. The dominant is the most common key to which to modulate when the tune is major.

The method is simple—get the new *doh* into your head, and think in that key. If, for example, you are in the key of D and wish to modulate in the second phrase, sing A, the dominant, at the end of the first phrase and imagine it as *doh*. Sing a few notes round this *doh* to get it firmly established. Then sing your second phrase in the new key, and solfa it in the new key after it is securely in your head. Apply this method to the first two phrases of ' Polly Oliver.'

Fig. 88   Polly Oliver

In Fig. 89 the change feels as if it occurs about the middle of the third phrase, at *.

Fig. 89   The blue bells of Scotland

When changing key (at present) always aim for a perfect cadence in the new key, and end on *doh*. See Figs. 88 and 89 above.

Avoid the use of *fah* (of the old key) when you are about to modulate, as it does not belong to the new key. It may be a help to aim for the new sound (*fe*, becoming *te*), but there is no need for it to be present in the tune. When it is absent we say the modulation is 'implied.'

Fig. 90

The Vicar of Bray

Key A

When modulation is 'implied' the most common cadence is for the melody to fall by step to the tonic as in Fig. 90. Fig. 91 does this in a decorated form.

Fig. 91

The Old Woman and the Pedlar

1st time

2nd time

Key A

If the first and second phrases of a four-phrase tune are identical, or nearly so, then the modulation will occur in the third phrase. Otherwise the most usual place is the second phrase.

In order to sound complete the tune must return to the tonic key and it is often easier and more natural to do this immediately, i.e., at the beginning of the next phrase. When making the return, think once more in the original key. Analyse Figs. 88-91 to see where each tune returns to the tonic.

Exercise XXXII. Add a complementary phrase to each of the following, ending in the dominant key. Work each example twice, the first time with the modulation expressed, the second time with it implied.

Fig. 92

Exercise XXXIII. Complete the following to make 8 or 16 bar tunes, each having a modulation to the dominant and a return to the original key.

Fig. 93

19   Modulation to the Relative Major

When in a minor key, the most common modulation is to the relative major. The process is exactly the same as that outlined in the last paragraph. Realise what notes are different in the two keys before you start. The relative major requires no accidentals. Fig. 94 begins and ends in E minor, while the second phrase and half the third is in G major.

Fig. 94   David of the White Rock

Exercise XXXIV. Add a complementary phrase to each of the following, ending in the relative major key.

Fig. 95

Exercise XXXV. Complete the following to make 8 or 16 bar tunes, each modulating to the relative major and back.

Fig. 96

20 Melodies for a Definite Medium

Thus far melodies have not been thought of as being written for any particular voice or instrument. But frequently it is necessary or advisable to write for a definite medium.

An instrumental melody is often of a more rhythmic nature than a vocal one, and repeated notes are more frequently used. Leaps may be wider and more frequent, as long as they sound well. Your teacher may even allow you to use an occasional augmented interval !

Marks of phrasing and expression should now be used. If a melody is phrased by means of slurs, staccato dots, *sforzando* marks, etc., or if it is bowed for a stringed instrument, there is no need to insert larger phrase marks to show the structure, unless you are particularly told to do so.

A melody for violin or piano can have a wider range than a vocal one and for this reason may often have a better climax.

Fig. 97

Violin melody from Finale of
G minor Symphony. Mozart

Exercise XXXVI. Complete the following, to make melodies as indicated.

Fig. 98

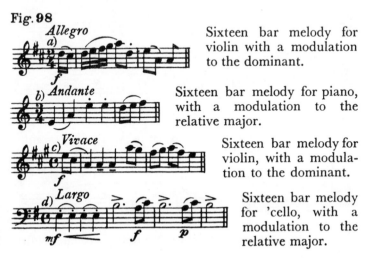

Sixteen bar melody for violin with a modulation to the dominant.

Sixteen bar melody for piano, with a modulation to the relative major.

Sixteen bar melody for violin, with a modulation to the dominant.

Sixteen bar melody for 'cello, with a modulation to the relative major.

21   Additional Exercises

Remember that a good tune requires the right balance between unity and variety. It must never meander aimlessly, and it must be thought of in terms of musical ideas, not just notes.

Rhythm. For the purposes of development a rhythmic figure is of more value than a melodic one. A rhythmic pattern repeated with the melody changed is more like the original than is a melody repeated with the rhythm changed.

Therefore analyse the rhythmic figures of the given opening with the idea of using these later in the tune. Quite often A, as well as being used as a whole, can be split up into two or more sections which can be developed separately.

Fig. 99

Let B be a good rhythmic contrast to A. If, for example, A is slow moving, let B be quicker, and vice versa.

Fig. 100

Or, if A has quavers, B might use a dotted crotchet figure or vice versa.

Fig. 101

Do not use the same rhythmic figure too often, particularly in the case of dotted figures. After using it once or twice either develop it or provide it with a contrast. On the other hand beware of a fussy rhythm, with too many notes, and too many changes of time pattern.

Development of a rhythmic figure can often be made to help towards a climax. For example, a figure containing a few quavers can make greater use of them later (see second half of Fig. 101), or the quicker moving part of a figure can be used continuously for a few beats, thus heightening the tension.

Fig. 102

Pitch. The developments of stepwise figures usually remain stepwise, though they may run on different notes or in the opposite direction. See Fig. 101.

Leaps, as for example, the notes of a chord in arpeggio, should remain as leaps when developed, but the size of the intervals may be changed, perhaps to fit another chord or to work towards a climax.

Fig. 103

If A uses leaps it may be wise to let B run stepwise, and vice versa. See Fig. 103.

Phrasing. The subdivision of phrases helps to make a tune shapely and to provide development within the phrase. See Figs. 99, 101, 102 and 103. Also it is easier to think in small sections than in larger ones. The more notes you write in a bar, the more do you need to break up your phrases.

Cadences. Each phrase must come to rest at a clearly defined cadence, and for those whose rhythmic sense is not strong it is advisable to make the cadences masculine.

Exercise XXXVII. Complete the following tunes according to the instructions given. You may divide up your phrases more than is indicated if you wish.

Fig. 104

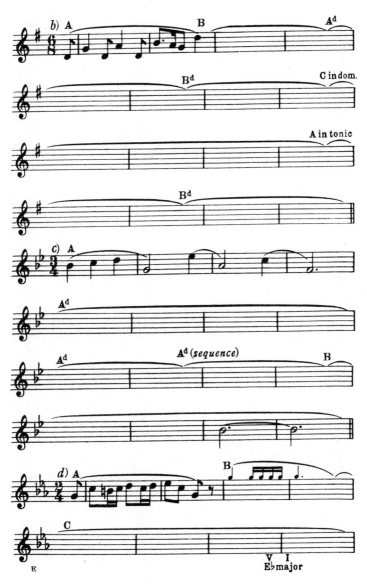

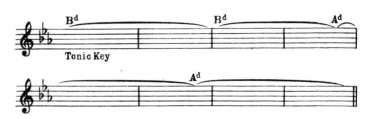

Exercise XXXVIII. Complete the following to make eight bar tunes on a scheme of your own.

Fig.**105**

Exercise XXXIX. Complete the following to make twelve bar tunes on a scheme of your own.

Fig.**106**

Exercise XL. Complete the following to make sixteen bar tunes on a scheme of your own. Each tune should include one modulation.

Fig.**107**

PART II

THE SETTING OF WORDS TO A MELODY: REGULAR, SHORT STANZAS

Before working Sections 1–7, Sections 1–5 of Part I should have been studied and the student should be able to write in compound time.

1   Words of One Syllable

Before setting a complete stanza to music our attention must first be directed to words. There are also certain rules concerned with the notation of words and music that must be learnt.

Each syllable must be written *exactly* under the note for which it is intended. This usually means that the notes have to be written further apart than usual, in order not to cramp long syllables such as 'through'. It is as well to get into the habit of wide spacing whenever words are being set to music. Also take care not to write the words too close to the stave above, otherwise when notes are written below the stave they will get in the way and make it impossible to write the words in a straight line.

Notes which are normally joined together in instrumental music, because they belong to the same beat, should be separated in vocal writing if they belong to different words or syllables. For example :—

Remember you are writing for a singer and keep within the range of his or her voice. Sometimes it is harder to sing a song which lies rather high all the time than to sing one which lies lower on the whole but has a few really high notes. Avoid a leap to a high note on an unimportant syllable and avoid also high notes on awkward vowels. If you find your

47

tune has risen too high you can always transpose it afterwards.

Exercise I. Write a tune to these words, using the given rhythms. Put each word exactly under its own note, and separate the stems where necessary.

(a) Crack goes the whip, and through the streets we go.

(b) The birds do call and sing ; how gay is the spring.

(c) Down by the brook lived a small wee elf.

(d) Sing a song of May time, O sing of May.

(e) She did not say to the sun, Good Night,
Though she saw him there like a ball of light.

(Houghton)

2 Words of More Than One Syllable

Words that split into two or more syllables require at least one note to each syllable. Each syllable must be written exactly under its own note and separated from the other syllables by a hyphen. The note may not be joined to another note even though it is part of the same word or beat. For example :—

From Hel - i - con's har - mon - ious springs A
thou - sand rills their ma - zy pro - gress take.

(*Gray*)

The correct division of words into syllables sometimes

causes difficulty, yet it is important if the singer is to grasp the meaning quickly. A knowledge of grammar is a help in analysing the structure of a word, particularly a knowledge of prefixes and suffixes. 'Pre', 'ad', 'ex', 'de', 'in', 'un', ' dis', ' bi' are common prefixes ; 'ly', 'ed', 'ing', 'ious', 'ate', 'er', 'est', 'age', 'ness', 'ment' are common suffixes, and they should usually be treated as complete syllables.

A knowledge of Latin is also helpful in dividing up a word ; e.g., in-cant-a-tion, con-son-ant.

A consonant after a long vowel should usually be placed at the beginning of the next syllable, whereas a short vowel usually requires its following consonant in the same syllable.

E.g., dī-late, dĭs-tance, bā-by, băb-oon. If, however, a mute ' e ' follows the consonant both letters should be in the same syllable as the preceding vowel. E.g., ex-cite-ment. You may cause misreading by faulty division. E.g., if you write ' sil ' as the first syllable in ' silent ' you may cause your singer to sound rather ' sil-ly ' !

Dipthongs should not be split, but two separate vowel sounds following one another (a comparative rarity in the English language) require two separate notes. Compare 'speed', 'fault', with 'ae-o-lian', 'be-at-if-ic'.

Many sounds in the English language are elided, and others are said so lightly that an unnatural effect is caused if one tries to sing a separate note to them. E.g., ' flower ' is better sung as one syllable. Notice also 'fier-y', 'pit-eous'.

The ' e ' in such words as ' crowned ' is mute, as spoken and sung today, but in classical poetry one sometimes meets ' crown-ed ' as two syllables, or ' crown'd ' if only one is intended.

Repeated consonants are usually split. E.g., ham-mer, bel-lows, sor-row. But this is not done if the word might thereby be mispronounced. Compare ' fall-ing ' (not ' fal-ling ') with ' trip-ping.'

Two different consonants are usually split also. E.g., gob-let, wan-der, lin-ger, fan-cy. But ' mount-ain ' is better than ' moun-tain ' because mount is a separate word.

Where three or more consonants come together the division will probably depend upon the points already mentioned. E.g., Lit-tle (repeated consonant) ; be-strewn (prefix) ; strength-en (suffix) ; en-chant-ment (prefix and suffix) ; land-scape (two words).

A silent consonant must not be separated from a vowel or consonant with which it is associated. E.g., e-cho ; whis-tle, en-thuse, per-fec-tion. ' Ec-ho,' ' ent-huse ' would be mispronounced.

Study the division of words into syllable in the musical examples given in Part IV.

Exercise II. Divide these words into syllables :—

Summer, every, hillocks, hollow, labour, spangle, tender, hawthorn, nibbling, enthroned, neighbour, untwisted, thoroughly, violet, procrastination, absurdity, shadowy, wonderful, consolation, solitude, adversity, generous, migration, dominion, pioneer, prayerful, heavenly, encasement.

Exercise III. Write tunes to the following words, using the given rhythms. Put each syllable exactly under its own note, separating the notes where necessary. There is one note for each syllable.

(a) Home for the holidays, here we go ;
    Bless me, the train is exceedingly slow. (Eliza Cook)

(b) Every night my prayers I say,
    And get my dinner every day. (Stevenson)

(c) Under a spreading chestnut tree
    The village smithy stands. (Longfellow)

(d) So daring in love and so dauntless in war,
   Have ye e'er heard of gallant like young Lochinvar.
                                                    (Scott)

d)
$\frac{3}{4}$ ♩ | ♩ ♩ ♩ | ♩ ♫ | ♩ | ♩ ♩ ♩ | ♩ ♫ | ♩ ♩ ♩ | ♩. ♩ | ♩ ♩ ♩ | ♩ | ♩ ‖

(e) They never were ill or at all dejected ;
   By all admired and by some respected.   (Lear)

e)
$\frac{6}{8}$ ♪ | ♫ ♫ ♩. ♫ | ♩ | ♪ ♫ ♫ | ♩ | ♪ ♩ ♫ | ♩ | ♪ ♫ ‖

(f) Thank goodness we shan't have to study and stammer
   Over Latin and sums and that nasty French grammar!
                                                (Eliza Cook)

f)
$\frac{6}{8}$ ♪ | ♫ ♪, ♪ ♫ ♫. ♪ | ♫ ♫. ♪ ♫ ♫ ♪ | ♫ ♫ ♫ ♫ | ♫ ♫. ♫ ‖

3 Verbal Accent

Words, whether in poetry or prose, carry their own
accentuation and therefore, to a large extent, dictate the
time pattern of your tune. Such words as 'an', 'to', 'of',
'by', etc., are weak syllables and must therefore not come
on an accent in music. Words of two or more syllables
always have one syllable more accented than another.

You would never say ' bé-cause ' ; therefore, in setting
this word, ' cause ' must be sung on a stronger accent than
' be ' and there may even be a bar line between the two
syllables.

Say the following words with the accent as marked, then
say them with the accent in a different place and hear how
wrong they sound :—

Miráculous, infallibílity, interférence, géntleman.

Notice that all the above words have more than one accent,
but that these accents are not all equally strong. The
strongest accent is the one marked.

Exercise IV. Divide these words into syllables, putting an
accent mark over the strongest syllable :—

Between, morning, intensely, disappoint, beautiful,
indescribable, immemorial, myriad, murmuring, obscurest,

melancholy, gardener, present (noun), present (verb), consent, enchantment.

4 Metrical Accent

In words, as in music, an accent comes every two or three sounds. (With four or more syllables or notes there are always two or more accents, though they may not be equally strong.) This means that if the accent is regular, as in verse, the pattern must be: /◡; ◡/; /◡◡; ◡/◡; or ◡◡/.

These five kinds of metrical 'feet' are illustrated below :—

(a) Trochaic.

/ ◡ / ◡ / ◡ / (◡)
Piping down the valleys wild
/ ◡ / ◡ / ◡ / (◡)
Piping songs of pleasant glee. (Blake)

(b) Iambic.

◡ / ◡ / ◡ / ◡ /
I wandered lonely as a cloud
◡ / ◡ / ◡ / ◡ /
That floats on high o'er vales and hills.
(Wordsworth)

(c) Dactylic.

/ ◡ ◡ / ◡ ◡ / ◡ ◡ / (◡◡)
How do you like to go up in a swing. (Stevenson)

(d) Amphibrachic.

◡ / ◡ ◡ / ◡ ◡ / ◡ ◡ /
The lights from the parlour and kitchen shone out
◡ ◡ / ◡ ◡ / ◡ ◡ /
Through the blinds and the windows and bars.
(Stevenson)

(e) Anapaestic.

◡ ◡ / ◡ ◡ / ◡ ◡ /
I am out of humanity's reach
◡ ◡ / ◡ ◡ / ◡ ◡ /
I must finish my journey alone. (Cowper)

(N.B. Marks dividing the feet from each other are purposely not shown, as they may be confused with bar lines, whereas their purpose is quite different.)

Notice that the last foot of a line often consists of only one syllable, particularly in trochaic and dactylic metres. This is called a truncated foot.

Exercise V. Add accent marks to the following, thereby showing that you recognise the metre :—

    (a) There lived a sage in days of yore
        And he a handsome pigtail wore.   (Thackeray)

    (b) Where the pools are bright and deep,
        Where the grey trout lies asleep.   (Hogg)

    (c) Home from the Indies, and home from the ocean ;
        Heroes and soldiers, we all shall come home.
                                   (Stevenson)

    (d) Jenny kissed me when we met,
        Jumping from the chair she sat in.   (Leigh Hunt)

    (e) ' My stars', cried the mouse, while his eye beamed
           with glee ;
        ' Here's a treasure I've found ; what a feast it will be''.
                                (Eliza Cook)

    (f) ' Tis the voice of the sluggard ; I heard him complain
        ' You have waked me too soon ; I must slumber again'.
                                (Isaac Watts)

5 Musical Accent and Rhythm

In setting verse to melody there is not bound to be a bar line before every accented syllable. Words which demand a jerky or disjointed style may work best with one metrical foot to the bar, but a smoother flow will be produced by writing two feet to a bar.

It must be remembered that there is often more than one accent to a bar, for *accent in music is relative.* It is true that the first beat of a bar usually carries the strongest accent. But the first of a pair of quavers on any beat of the bar is stronger than the second   (♩♩) , and the third of four semiquavers is stronger than the second and fourth, though not as strong as the first. (♩♩♩♩)

Notice the relative strength of the accents in the following :

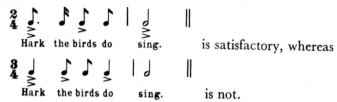

Suppose the words ' Hark, the birds do sing ' are to be set to a rhythm lasting two bars. The first and last words carry the strongest accents; and should therefore have bar lines before them. | Hark, the birds do | sing ||. But ' birds ' also has an accent and must be sung on a stronger part of the bar than the ' the ' and 'do'. Therefore

is satisfactory, whereas

is not.

Lines beginning with a weak syllable will obviously require an anacrusic rhythm, but sometimes even a line beginning with a strong syllable, may not start on the first beat of the bar. E.g.,

A ⁴₄ rhythm using a fair number of short notes can easily carry two metrical feet to the bar, and ⁴₄ nearly always does so.

When a triple rhythm is desired ⁶₈ is very useful. It has less frequent strong accents than ³₄ and is therefore more flowing. Compare

with

Many songs in ¾ time would be more correctly written in ⁶₈, as the composer did not intend an equally strong accent at the beginning of every bar.

A beginner does not always realise the varieties of time pattern that are possible in setting metrical feet. He tends to write feet with two syllables always in ²₄ time and feet with three syllables always in ¾ time and to write mainly, if not entirely, in crotchets.

Carefully compare the following rhythms, all of which will fit to the same line of words, though the two bar rhythms fit better than the four bar ones.

Compare also :—

The following setting has faulty accents within the bar, though the bar lines are in the right places.

Be - side   a green mea - dow   a stream used to   flow.

'Patter' songs are a special variety of song which use quick notes with very little variety of note length, though even here the accent must be correct. But most other types of songs gain by having varied note lengths which enhance the subtlety of the words.

Another way of getting variety is to write two or more notes to one syllable (the melisma). This is shown by joining them if they belong to the same beat and by writing a slur above or below if they cannot be joined. E.g.,

Be - side   a   green   mea - dow a   stream used to   flow.

Some publishers print a slur even when the stems can be joined ; they would slur the quavers on 'green' in the example above. And it is customary to put a dash after the syllable to show its extent. See 'like' in Fig. 1.

Handel and other classical composers made great use of the melisma. Fig. 1 shows Parry getting an ecstatic feeling into 'My heart is like a singing bird' by this means.

heart is like_ a rain-bow shell That pad-dles in a pur - ple_ sea; My heart is gladder than all these Be- -cause_____ my love is come_____ to me!

Study also the rhythmic setting of the words of the Parry songs quoted in Part IV, Figs. 6 and 8 .

Exercise VI. Write tunes to the following words. Work thus :—

(1) Mark the accents.
(2) Put in the bar lines. There should be two or four to every line in order to produce normal phrase lengths.
(3) Write note lengths over each syllable.

(4) Clothe the rhythm with a tune, writing it out as you were shown in Sections 1 and 2. Realise that very frequently the end of the first line and the beginning of the second will be in the same bar.

(a) Sing lullaby, as women do,
Wherewith they bring their babe to rest. (Gascoigne)
(b) Come live with me and be my love
And we will all the pleasures prove. (Marlowe)
(c) There is a garden in her face
Where roses and white lilies blow. (Campion)
(d) Amarantha sweet and fair
Ah, braid no more that shiny hair. (Lovelace)
(e) Rain may keep raining, and others go roam,
But I can be happy and building at home.
(Stevenson)
(f) And as long as I live and where'er I may be
I'll always remember my town by the sea.
(Stevenson)

6   Lines Containing a Variety of Metrical Feet

It is quite customary for a stanza to contain different kinds of metrical feet. Sometimes an occasional foot may be of a different variety, as in the following, where the first foot is dactylic while the others are trochaic :—

> Love is the blossom, where there blows
> Everything that lives or grows.   (Fletcher)

Sometimes the lines are so mixed that it is impossible to say which is the prevailing rhythm. E.g. :—

> Surely they should not pass their lives
> Without any chance of husbands or wives !

> (Lear)

Sometimes a complete line is changed. E.g. :—

> It was a lover and his lass (Iambic)
> With a hey and a ho and a hey nonino (Anapaestic)
> (Shakespeare)

Sometimes the second half of a verse or a chorus changes its rhythm, as in Shakespeare's 'Blow, blow thou winter wind'.

As long as you are alert and can feel the changes when they occur there is no difficulty in setting such stanzas to music, for the note lengths within the bar can be varied at will.

Exercise VII.   Write rhythms or melodic phrases to the following, working as in Ex. VI :—

(1) They whistled and warbled a moony song
     To the echoing sound of a coppery gong.   (Lear)
(2) Sir Ralph bent over the boat
     And he cut the bell from the Inchcape float. (Southey)
(3) There let us walk, there let us play,
     Through the meadows, among the hay.   (Hogg)
(4) There were three sailors of Bristol City
     Who took a boat and went to sea.   (Thackeray)

7 Metrical Accents On Unaccented Syllables

Anyone with a feeling for rhythm is aware that sometimes a metrical accent falls on a weak syllable. Some means must be found of avoiding a musical accent at such places. Compare the following :—

(*a*) Produces a false accent at 'in'; (*b*) avoids it by means of a tied note and (*c*) uses a rest.

Study the skilful avoidance of false accents and the subtlety of the rhythm in Fig. 2.

Fig. 2 *Lento dolente*   A Dirge.   Walford Davies

Exercise VIII.   Write rhythms or melodic phrases to the following, working as before :—

(a) Love not me for comely grace
     For my pleasing eye or face.   (Anon)

(b) Sweet, be not proud of those two eyes
     Which, starlike, sparkle in their skies.   (Herrick)

(c) Piper sit thee down and write
     In a book that all may read.   (Blake)

(d) It was a summer evening
     Old Kaspar's work was done.   (Southey)

(e) The boat is lowered, the boat men row,
     And to the Inchcape rock they go.   (Southey)

(f) A gown made of the finest wool
     Which from our pretty lambs we pull.   (Marlowe)

8   The Silent Foot. Ballad Metre
Read and work Part 1, Section 9.

The commonest metre in the English language is probably the ballad metre.   This consists of an Iambic tetrameter (line of 4 feet) followed by an Iambic trimeter (line of 3 feet), repeated to make a 4-line stanza.   But anyone reading verse in this metre consciously or unconsciously adds an extra silent foot at the end of the trimeter line.   Notice this as you read the following :—

> O wha is this has done this deed
> Has tauld the King o' me
> To send us out this time of the year
> To sail upon the sea ?

In setting this rhythm to music you must write a long note or a rest to account for this silent foot, otherwise your musical phrase will sound wrong too, and you will not get regular two and four bar phrases.

Tetrameters followed by trimeters are common with other kinds of feet besides Iambic, though the verse is not then in ' ballad metre'.

Exercise IX.   Write rhythms or melodic phrases to the following, working as before :—

(a) Fair daffodils we weep to see
   You haste away so soon.   (Herrick)

(b) Tell me not of a face that's fair
   Nor lip nor cheek that's red.   (Brome)

(c) Ding a dong, ding a dong, if you're pleased with my
     song
   I will feed you with cold apple tart.   (Lear)

(d) The King sits in Dunfermline town
   Drinking the bluid red wine.   (Ballad)

(e) He harnessed himself by the clear moonshine
   And he mounted his horse at the door.   (Kingsley)

(f) For the moon never beams without bringing me
     dreams
   Of the beautiful Annabel Lee.   (Poe)

9   Feminine Endings

Read and work Part 1, Section 13.

Every time that a line ends with a weak syllable a feminine ending is produced. The rhythm of the words should help you to decide the relative length of the last two or three notes, but be sure that the last strong syllable is on a stronger musical accent than the weak syllable or syllables which follow it. Compare the following :—

(a) is obviously wrong ; (b) is satisfactory and so is (c), as it is possible to sing ' sor ' heavier than 'row'.

F

See also :—

'Harmony' has two weak syllables after the strong one and might also have been set thus :—

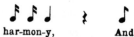

Exercise X. Write rhythms or melodic phrases to the following :—

(a) What was he doing, the great God Pan
Down in the reeds by the river ?   (E. B. Browning)

(b) It fell on a day and a bonnie simmer day
When green grew oats and barley.   (Ballad)

(c) Found in the garden, dead in his beauty,
O that a linnet should die in the spring.   (Ewing)

(d) They must never hope for glory
Their's is quite a different story.   (Stevenson)

(e) Where the blackbird sings the latest,
Where the hawthorn blooms the sweetest.   (Hogg)

10   The Four Line Stanza. Repetition and Development

Read and work Part 1, Sections 6–8.

So far, in the setting of words to music, the emphasis has been on the rhythm, and it is as well to devote your full attention to this at first.

Now, however, you are to set four line stanzas and you will have to give more thought to the melodic content of the music. Students who can write shapely tunes without words sometimes seem to forget all they have learnt about unity and variety, repetition, development, and sequence, when they come to set words to music, presumably because they are so pre-occupied with the words. It is true that a tune can stand more variety if it is to be sung to a number of verses than if it is to be heard only once. But most tunes, even to repeated verses, sound more shapely if they contain some repetition or development.

Therefore study the words to be set and decide which lines ' pair off' and could use the same or a similar tune. Sometimes you will feel that the rhyming lines go best together, sometimes the number of feet in a line provide the similarity and sometimes it is the sense that makes lines pair together.

In the following stanzas letters are placed at the beginning of the lines to show how they might be paired, though they are not, of course, bound to be set in this way.

A	My heart is like a singing bird
B	Whose nest is in a watered shoot ;
Ad	My heart is like an apple tree
Bd	Whose boughs are bent with thick set fruit.

(C. G. Rossetti)

A	Let us dance and let us sing
Ad	Dancing in a merry ring.
B	We'll be fairies on the green,
Bd	Sporting round the fairy queen. (Anon)

A	There was a little girl, and she wore a little curl
B	Right down the middle of her forehead.
C or Ad	When she was good she was very, very good
Bd	But when she was bad she was horrid. (Anon)

Do not worry if two lines that you think pair together have not exactly the same number of syllables in each line. You can easily vary the number of notes and the tune will still be a recognisable repetition or development of the earlier line—in fact, it may be all the better for the change. Compare the number of syllables in the second and fourth lines in the last stanza quoted above.

Perhaps you will feel now that you can compose a tune without thinking of the bar lines and the rhythm first. Try it and see whether what you have learnt in the preceding sections has borne fruit. In cases of doubt it may still, however, be wise to plan out the rhythm first, and the tune must always be checked afterwards for possible rhythmic weaknesses.

Exercise XI. Set the three stanzas quoted in Section 10, keeping to the plans suggested.

Exercise XII. Write melodies to the following stanzas, adding appropriate expression marks:—

> (a) Gather ye rosebuds while ye may,
>   Old time is still a flying ;
> And this same flower that smiles to-day
>   To-morrow will be dying.   (Herrick)

> (b) Where the hazel bank is steepest,
> Where the shadow falls the deepest,
> Where the clustering nuts fall free—
> That's the way for Billy and me.   (Hogg)

11 Verbal Significance and Rhythm

A study of the words to be set will often suggest the rhythm, the pace and phrasing of the tune. Obviously ' Faster than fairies, faster than witches', will want a quick disjointed style, while 'Lullaby, lullaby, sleep my baby dear', will want a slow legato setting.

Notice also the commas in the two lines quoted above. In ' faster than fairies, faster than witches ' the phrase obviously breaks into two sections, and the second section will probably repeat or develop the first, perhaps using sequence. In ' lullaby, lullaby, sleep my baby dear ' the phrase will probably divide into two units and a section, and the second ' lullaby ' will repeat or develop the first.

Notice the phrasing at each ' tail ' in the following :—

> He had a tail, and she had a tail,
>> Both long and curling and fine ;
> And each said : ' Yours is the finest tail
>> In the world, excepting mine.'   (Anon)

The first line obviously splits into sections, the second one being a repetition or development of the first. But ' tail ' at the end of the third line must have no pause, but must run straight on to the first three words of the next line. Beware of automatically making a pause at the end of every line, whether the sense requires it or not. See Fig. 3.

Fig. 3

Exercise XIII.   Write melodies to the following, adding appropriate expression marks :—

> (a) Faster than fairies, faster than witches,
> Bridges and houses, hedges and ditches ;
> And charging along like troops in a battle,
> All through the meadows the horses and cattle.
>> (Stevenson)

> (b) Charm me asleep and melt me so
> With thy delicious numbers
> That, being ravished, here I go
> Away in easy slumbers.   (Herrick)

> (c) How do you like to go up in a swing !
> Up in the air so blue ?
> Oh, I do think it the pleasantest thing
> Ever a child can do !   (Stevenson)

(d) ' Come back ! Come back ! ' he cried in grief,
    ' Across this stormy water ;
    And I'll forgive your highland chief,
    My daughter !—O my daughter ! '   (Campbell)

12 Verbal Significance and Melody

The words also frequently suggest the style of the melody and the rise and fall it requires. The inexperienced tune writer sometimes lets the melody get the upper hand and go its own way without reference to the words, perhaps rising to a climax on such words as ' and sink me down to rest ' ! Therefore study the words beforehand and decide where you think the climax should come.

Occasionally it may happen that the emotional climax of the words does not want a high note. In such a case a pause or a dramatic fall of the tune may still give the sense of climax.

Some words want a tune full of leaps (see Fig. 4), while others may want a tune that hardly rises or falls at all (see Fig. 5). Some may want a gay tune that swings along easily (see Fig. 6) ; while others want a smooth legato melody (see Fig. 7—the translation is responsible here for rising to the word ' repose ').

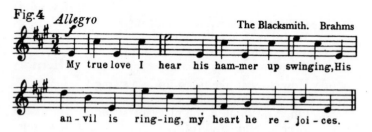

Fig. 4 *Allegro*   The Blacksmith. Brahms

Exercise XIV. Write tunes to the following, making them as expressive of the words as possible :—

(a) No stir in the air, no stir in the sea,
The ship was still as she could be.
Her sails from heaven received no motion,
Her keel was steady in the ocean. (Southey)

(b) Sound, sound the clarion, fill the fife !
To all the sensual world proclaim,
One crowded hour of glorious life
Is worth an age without a name. (Scott)

(c) He comes in the night, he comes in the night,
     He softly silently comes
     While the little brown heads on the pillows so white
     Are dreaming of bugles and drums.   (Anon)

(d) On we rode, the others and I
     Over the mountains blue, and by
     The silver river, the sounding sea
     And the robber woods of Tartary.   (Stevenson)

13 Other Common Metres to which Regular Two and Four Bar Phrases can be Written

So far all the stanzas you have set have had four metrical feet to a line or four and three feet in alternate lines. But there are many other possibilities. Lines of two feet are quite common and probably two such lines will form a phrase in music. Three feet lines usually want a silent bar at the end ; six feet lines are not very common and they too usually ask for silent bars to turn them into regular two and four bar phrases ; seven feet lines are nearly always the four plus three feet found in ballad metre ; and eight feet lines (which are rather rare) are merely a doubled four. Therefore lines of two, three, four, six, seven and eight feet can usually be set quite easily in a regular two or four bar musical rhythm.

The exception is the five foot line (the pentameter) and pentameters are common in English rhymed poetry as well as in blank verse. They are rare in lyric poetry, however, and are not often set to music. As they are more difficult to set they will be left until Part IV of this book.

The three most frequent metres to be found in regular hymns are long metre (LM), 8+8+8+8 syllables, 4+4+4+4 feet ; common metre (CM), 8+6+8+6 syllables, 4+3+4+3 feet—cf. ballad metre ; and short metre (SM), 6+6+8+6 syllables, 3+3+4+3 feet. Common metre and short metre make use of the silent foot.

Exercise XV. Write tunes to the following, using regular two and four bar phrases :—

(a) 2+2+2+2+2+2+2+2

    The year's at the spring
    And day's at the morn ;
    Morning's at seven ;
    The hillside's dew pearled ;
    The lark's on the wing ;
    The snail's on the thorn ;
    God's in his heaven—
    All's right with the world.   (R. Browning)

(b) 2+2+3+2+2+3

    There was one little Jim,
    'Tis reported of him
    And must be to his lasting disgrace,

    That he never was seen
    With hands at all clean
    Nor yet ever clean was his face.   (J. Taylor)

(c) 2+2+4+2+2+4

    Bird of the wilderness,
    Blithesome and cumberless,
    Sweet be thy matin o'er moorland and lea !
    Emblem of happiness,
    Blest is thy dwelling place
    Oh, to abide in the desert with thee !

                        (James Hogg)

(d) 3+3+3+3

    It was Earl Haldan's daughter
    She looked across the sea ;
    She looked across the water
    And long and loud laughed she.   (Kingsley)

(e) 3+3+4+3
> Who has seen the wind ?
> Neither I nor you.
> But when the leaves hang trembling
> The wind is passing thro'. (C. Rossetti)

(f) 6+6+6+6
> I will make you brooches and toys for your delight
> Of bird song at morning and star shine at night.
> I will make a palace fit for you and me
> Of green days in forests and blue days at sea.
>
> (Stevenson)

(g) 7+7+7+7
The more you work, the more you sing, the more the
  bellows roar ;
The falling stars, the flying sparks, stream shining more and
  more.
You hit so hard, you look so hot, and yet you never tire ;
It must be very nice to be allowed to play with fire !

(J. H. Ewing)

(h) 8+8+8+8
' Will you walk a little faster', said the whiting to the snail
' There's a porpoise close behind me, and he's treading on
  my tail.
See how eagerly the lobsters and the turtles all advance.
They are waiting on the shingle—will you come and join
  the dance ? ' (Lewis Carroll)

Exercise XVI. Try to find a song by a modern British
composer in each of the metres given in Exercise XV. Then
make a careful study of the composer's rhythm and phrasing.

Exercise XVII. Set the following as hymn tunes, writing
with minims as beats and separating the lines of words by
double bar lines :—

(a) LM.

> By, by, lullay before Him sing ;
> Go, wind the horn and pluck the string
> Till all the place with music ring ;
> And bid one prayer to Christ the King.   (Anon)

(b) CM.

> With joy approach, O Christian wight,
> Do homage to thy King
> And highly prize His humble pomp
> Which He from heaven doth bring.   (Southwell)

(c) SM.

> O ruler of the sky,
> Rule Thou within my heart :
> O great Adorner of the world
> Thy light of life impart.   (Lynch)

PART III

MORE ADVANCED MELODY WRITING

1 Binary Form

When a melody divides into two equal or approximately equal halves it is said to be in Binary Form—though the term is not generally used for a melody of less than sixteen bars.

Musical shape is very much linked up with modulation, and the following types of Binary Form will be found :—

(1) 1st half tonic key : 2nd half dominant returning to tonic.

(2) 1st half tonic modulating to dominant : 2nd half tonic.

(3) 1st half tonic modulating to dominant : 2nd half dominant returning to tonic.

If the melody is in the minor key then the modulation will probably be to the relative major.

The second half frequently repeats or develops some part of the first half. Sometimes the openings of the two halves correspond, and sometimes their endings are similar, apart from differences of key.

Fig.1   Openings Correspond   Du bist wie eine Blüme.   Schumann

Fig. 2   Endings Correspond   Serenade. Beethoven

Exercise I. Complete the following to make Binary Form melodies. Work each beginning three times, thus :—

(1) 1st half tonic key (it can end with a perfect cadence) : 2nd half touching on the complementary key and returning to the tonic. Use some repetition or development.

(2) 1st half tonic modulating to the complementary key : 2nd half tonic, the ends of each half being identical except for the change of key.

(3) 1st half tonic modulating to the complementary key : 2nd half starting in the complementary key, with the opening idea transposed, and returning to the tonic (with a similar ending if you wish).

Fig. 3   *a)* for piano   *b)* for violin

c) for contralto   *d)* for violin

2 Ternary Form

When a melody divides into three equal or approximately equal parts and the third part is a restatement of the first while the middle section provides contrast, it is said to be Ternary.

The first section may end with a perfect cadence in the tonic key and in that case its repetition at the end can be identical and need not be written out. The disadvantage of this plan is that it gives two perfect cadences in the tonic key. See Fig. 4.

The alternative plan is to end the first section in the complementary key. It will then have to be modified at its repetition in order to end in the tonic key. See Fig. 5.

The middle section usually begins in or modulates to the complementary key. It may end in that key with a perfect cadence, and this is the normal procedure when the modulation is to the dominant. See Fig. 6.

In the case of a minor tune, however, the middle section may end with the dominant chord of the tonic key instead of staying in the relative major, as this produces the desire to return to the opening. See Fig. 4.

National songs in ternary form are rare, as the verses usually consist of four or eight lines.

Fig. 4

Charlie is my darling

C minor

Eb major

V—

C minor

Exercise II. Take the beginnings given in Ex. I and write melodies in ternary form.

3 Hybrid Forms

Although the words binary and ternary are convenient terms do not imagine that every short piece must be one or the other. All sorts of combinations and lengths are possible, and as long as the shape is clear and balanced the terms themselves do not matter very much. What, for example, are we to call 'The Vicar of Bray' (AABA) in which we clearly hear four phrases, although the idea is ternary ; or Schumann's 'Merry Peasant' in which A, 4 bars, is repeated, then B, 2 bars, and A, 4 bars, are repeated as a second half (see Fig. 7), or pieces like Fig. 8 in which the length is again binary but the repetition at bar 13 creates a feeling of ternary ? Perhaps the simplest method is to avoid the use of these terms altogether in such pieces.

Exercise III. Take the beginnings given in Ex. I and write melodies which are binary in proportions but ternary in idea.

4   Melodies of Five and Seven Phrases

Sometimes tunes will be found consisting of five or seven phrases instead of the more usual four or six.

Analyse the following :—

Fig. 9   The Meeting of the Waters

Fig. 10   Hedge Roses.   Schubert

Exercise IV. Complete the following, to make (a) 5 phrase melodies ; (b) 7 phrase melodies. Add phrasing and expression marks.

Fig. 11
a) for piano

b) for contralto voice

G

5 Cadence Extension

Sometimes a regular-phrased tune is extended at the end by means of augmentation or repetition of the cadence, or by adding a short coda.

See also 'Hark, hark the lark', and the slow movement of Beethoven's Fifth Symphony where the first sentence is extended by cadential repetition from eight bars to twenty-two.

Fig.14

Last Verse of " Two Brown Eyes "   Grieg

Coda

Exercise V. Take any tunes you have previously written and extend them by means of one of the ways shown above.

6   Phrase Extension

Sometimes a phrase is extended by means of an interpolation, or a sequence, or a long note in the middle of a phrase. Such an irregular phrase is usually in answer to a regular one, and forms a pleasant means of avoiding too much squareness.

Fig.15

Where are you going to, my pretty maid

extension by sequence

Fig.16

The Happy Lover

extension   augmentation

Fig. 17 *Andante* — Slow movement, Violin Concerto. Mendelssohn

extension

Exercise VI. Take any tunes you have previously written and extend one of the phrases (preferably the last) in one of the ways shown above.

7   Phrase Contraction

Sometimes a phrase is contracted by means of diminution, omission, or the end of one phrase overlapping with the beginning of the next. Such contraction will usually occur in an answering rather than an announcing phrase. Phrase contraction is much less common than phrase extension.

Fig. 18 *Andante* — Slow movement, Schubert Sonata in A

cadence contraction

Fig. 19 — Wandering Miller.   Schubert

Exercise VII. Take any tunes you have previously written and contract a phrase in one of the ways shown above.

8 Regular Phrases of Unusual Length

Sometimes phrases will be found which do not seem to contain any irregular extension or contraction, and yet which are not two or four bars long.

Fig.20 3+3+3+3   The Nightingale.   Brahms

Fig.21 6 :‖4+4+4‖   The Rising of the Lark

Fig.22 7+7+6   It was a lover and his lass

Exercise VIII. Continue the following fragments to make tunes on the given phrase plans :—

Fig.23

a) 3+3+6

b) 5+5+5+5

c) 6+4+6

d) 7+7, the tune being entirely your own.

It is important to realise that the normal phrase is two or four bars, and that the delight of hearing a three, five or seven bar phrase lies in its comparative rarity. Unless you have a very good sense of musical balance or unless you are required to write irregular phrases for examination purposes it will be wise to keep to regular ones most of the time.

9   Various Note Lengths as the Beat

Practice is needed in writing tunes with beats of various note lengths. The minim is normally the beat in a hymn tune ; ⅜ time is quite common ; ²₄, ⁶₄ and ⁹₁₆ will occasionally be found. Beethoven frequently uses a minim beat in his Allegros, and a quaver or dotted quaver beat in his slow movements, though the time signature does not always indicate this. E.g., he may write ²₄ when he means ⁴₈.

If you use time names as a help in writing down a tune remember to call the beat ' taa ' however it is written. E.g., in ⅜ time ♩ is taa-aa and ♫ is ta-te, while in ⁴₂ time ♩♩ is ta-te.

Exercise IX. Write tunes on the following rhythms. Add phrase marks to all except the first. (In hymn tunes a double bar line takes the place of phrase marks.)

Exercise X. Complete the following extracts to make tunes. They can be any length and shape you like.

10 Modulation to Other Related Keys

The most closely related keys to a given key centre are those which have not more than one sharp or flat different in the key signature.

From a major key centre these keys are the relative minor, the dominant major and its relative minor, the subdominant major and its relative minor.

From a minor key centre they are the relative major, the dominant minor and its relative major, the subdominant minor and its relative major.

The method of modulating to these keys is the same as that outlined for the dominant major.

Fig.26

Poor Old Horse

Eb major

Fig.27

Sing a Song of Sixpence

G minor

C minor

Exercise XI. Add another phrase to the following beginnings, modulating to each of the related keys in turn.

Fig.28

11 Key Schemes in Binary and Ternary Form

More complicated pieces in binary and ternary form may modulate to several keys. A good deal of freedom in key scheme is possible, though it is a general principle to modulate to the sharp side of the key first and the flat side later. The relative major or minor of the tonic may be used anywhere.

In a major key beware of using the subdominant major near the beginning, as it has a tendency to oust the tonic from its position of key centre. This may happen elsewhere too, if you stay in the subdominant key too long.

Establish the tonic key firmly and clearly at the beginning and return to it in time to re-establish it at the end.

As you get on to writing longer and more advanced melodies you will realise the value of your harmony lessons, for a good tune is usually just the surface of a good chord scheme. It is assumed that you are studying harmony at the same time as melody writing, and that you are, by now, familiar with good chord progressions. If you study modulation in harmony at the same time as modulation in melody you will find that each helps the other.

When writing a melody it is advisable sometimes to begin with the harmony rather than the melody and to make out a chord scheme complete with pivot chords and modulatory sequences, probably changing the chords only once or twice in a bar. You will find this particularly helpful if you have difficulty in feeling changes of key. Then write the tune over this chord scheme.

At other times you may like to try writing a complete accompaniment. A study of the chapter on accompaniment writing in Part III of Kitson's ' Elementary Harmony ' will be found very helpful in this connection. Although this is not a harmony book a few hints may be useful here. Do not change the chords too often and do not harmonise every note. Discords may resolve at a different octave and the texture may vary. One chord may have three notes in it and the following chord may have six. Experiment with a few broken chord figures, varying their rhythm after a few bars, and remember that consecutive 5ths and 8ves between the bass and an upper part rarely sound well, though they may sometimes be used elsewhere in piano writing.

In the remaining exercises in this part of the book, and also in Part IV you must always think harmonically. If you do not build on a complete chord scheme or there is no time to write an accompaniment, then, as a minimum, you should indicate the key changes and name the chords at each cadence. Only in this way will you keep ' on the rails ' and make your intentions clear to others. This has been done in the examples which follow.

Sections 12-16 suggest some good key schemes which may be followed until you get more experience.

12 Binary Form, Major Key

A   1st phrase : Tonic major.
 2nd phrase : Dominant major ; or through relative or mediant minor to dominant major.
B   3rd phrase : Tonic major ; or through tonic major to subdominant major or supertonic minor or both. Sequences are useful here.
 4th phrase : Tonic major, perhaps touching on the subdominant major or supertonic minor at the beginning of the phrase.

Fig. 29 illustrates the above scheme except that the first phrase modulates to the dominant and is then repeated for the second phrase.

Fig. 29 *Moderato*   Come let us all this day. Bach

Exercise XII. Complete the following, as indicated, in binary form, naming the keys and cadences as in Fig. 29, or building on a chord scheme, or adding an accompaniment. Add phrasing and expression marks.

Fig.30

a) Minuet for piano

Keys F major, C major, F major, B♭ major, G minor, F major.

b) Gigue for violin

Keys G major, E minor, D major, G major, C major, G major.

c) March for piano

Keys C major, E minor, G major, F major, D minor, C major.

13 Binary Form. Minor Key

A 1st phrase : Tonic minor.

2nd phrase : Relative major ; or through dominant to relative major ; or vice versa. If the phrase ends in the dominant minor key it may be wise to think of the last chord as being major (Picardy 3rd), as this is the dominant chord of the tonic key and the tune can then easily return to the tonic in the third phrase.

B   3rd phrase : May start in tonic, relative major or
dominant minor and may modulate to submediant
major or subdominant minor or both.
4th phrase : Tonic minor.

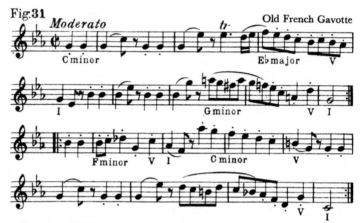

Fig.31   Moderato   tr.   Old French Gavotte

C minor   Eb major   V
I   G minor   V I
F minor   V I   C minor   V
V   I

Exercise XIII.   Complete the following, as indicated, in
binary form.   Follow the instructions given in Exercise XII.

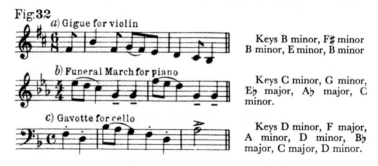

Fig.32   *a)* Gigue for violin

Keys B minor, F♯ minor
B minor, E minor, B minor

b) Funeral March for piano

Keys C minor, G minor,
Eb major, Ab major, C
minor.

c) Gavotte for cello

Keys D minor, F major,
A minor, D minor, Bb
major, C major, D minor.

14   Extended Binary Form

Binary form pieces are often found in which the second
half is considerably longer than the first.   In Fig. 33 A is ten
bars and B is sixteen bars, both parts containing extensions.

Fig. **33** *Allegro*   Gavotte.   Bach

Exercise XIV. Take some of the exercises already written in Exercises XII and XIII and rewrite them, extending them in the second half.

15   Ternary Form, Major Key

A   1st phrase : Tonic major.
  2nd phrase : Tonic major, or through the supertonic minor to the tonic major.
B   3rd phrase : Relative or mediant minor.
  4th phrase : Dominant major.
A   1st and 2nd phrases repeated.

Fig. 34

See the conquering hero comes.   Handel

Alternative Scheme.

A   1st phrase : Tonic major.
    2nd phrase : Dominant major or through relative or
    mediant minor to the dominant major.

B   3rd phrase : Subdominant major or supertonic minor
    or both.

    4th phrase : Subdominant major or supertonic or
    relative minor, leading to the dominant key or the
    dominant chord of the tonic key.

A   5th phrase : Repetition of first phrase in tonic major.
    6th phrase : Tonic major or through relative or
    supertonic minor to tonic major (may be a repeti-
    tion of the second phrase transposed).

Fig. 35

Träumerei.   Schumann

Exercise XV. Take the beginnings given in Exercise XII and write pieces in ternary form, making your own key scheme.

16   Ternary Form, Minor Key

A   1st phrase : Tonic minor.
   2nd phrase : Tonic minor or through subdominant minor to tonic minor.
B   3rd phrase : Relative or submediant major or subdominant minor.
   4th phrase : Any related key, leading to relative major or dominant minor.
A   1st and 2nd phrases repeated.
In Fig. 36 the B section is extended to twelve bars.

Fig. 36   Minuet. Handel

Alternative Scheme.

A 1st phrase : Tonic minor.
2nd phrase : To relative major or dominant minor.
B 3rd phrase : Any related key.
4th phrase : Any related key leading to dominant minor or dominant chord of tonic key.
A 5th phrase : As first phrase, tonic minor.
6th phrase : Tonic minor (may be a partial repetition of the second phrase, transposed).

Fig. 37

Trio from Sonata. Beethoven

Exercise XVI. Take the beginnings given in Ex. XIII and write pieces in ternary form, making your own key scheme.

17 Additional Exercise

1. Write a sixteen bar melody beginning thus. It must modulate to the dominant and the relative minor and must contain a sequence.

Fig. 38

2. Write a sixteen bar melody beginning thus. It must modulate to the relative major and one other related key, and must contain at least one example of development.

Fig. 39

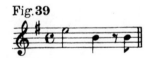

3. Add two bars to the opening given below ; then add a responsive phrase of five bars.

Fig. 40

4. Add two bars to the opening given below ; then add a responsive phrase of six bars.

Fig. 41

5. Write a melody beginning thus, consisting of three two-bar phrases.

Fig. 42

6. Write a melody in binary form beginning thus. It must modulate to three different related keys.

Fig. 43

H

7. Write a melody in ternary form beginning thus. It must modulate to three different related keys.

Fig.44

8. Write a twelve bar melody beginning thus. It must modulate to F minor, E♭ major and B♭ minor.

Fig.45

9. Complete the following melody :

Fig.46

10. Add an opening half to this melody :

Fig.47

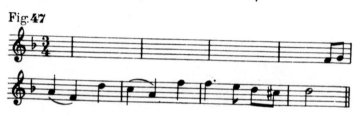

11. Write a gigue for violin in A major, modulating to the following keys : E major, A major, D major, F♯ minor, A major.

12. Write a bourrée for 'cello containing at least three modulations to related keys.

13. Write a minuet for piano in ternary form, showing some use of development.

14. Write a sixteen bar melody for violin, and add a simple piano accompaniment.

By the same author

HARMONY A Textbook for Class Use on Aural Foundations

A GRADED MUSIC COURSE Book 1
Book 2
Book 3

SCORE READING, FORM AND HISTORY
(Book 4)

ADDITIONAL SIGHT SINGING EXERCISES
READ, SING AND PLAY

Book 1 (Teachers' Edition)
(Pupils' Edition)

In preparation Book 2
Book 3
Book 4

PART IV

MORE ADVANCED MELODY WRITING TO WORDS

1 Stanzas of Five and Six Lines

Read and work Part 3, Section 4.

Perhaps the most common form of five line stanza is that in which there is a regular four lines with an extra line on the end rather like a coda (see Ex. I (a)). But 3+2 and 2+3 lines are also quite common (see Ex. I (b) and (c)), and 2+1+2 may occasionally be found (see Ex. I (d). It is not particularly difficult to write five phrases if each phrase is two or four bars in length, but take care that the tune hangs together well and avoid too finished a cadence at the end of the fourth line.

Six-line stanzas also occur in various forms. Sometimes they seem to fall into a ternary form, though the last two lines are usually better as a development than as an exact repetition of the first two (see Ex. II (a)). At other times they may make a binary form 3+3 (see Ex. II (b)). But sometimes one feels that a six line stanza is made so by means of extensions, as in Ex. II (c), (sequences are often helpful in such cases), and frequently the last two lines feel like a coda (see Ex. II (d)).

Study Fig. 1, which is an example of a very natural and rhythmical setting of a six line stanza. Notice the climax on ' builds ', making use of an earlier figure, and the extension at the end.

Fig. 1

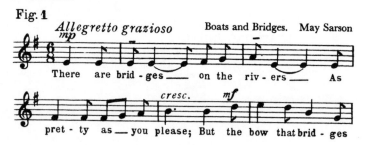

Allegretto grazioso Boats and Bridges. May Sarson

There are brid - ges ___ on the riv - ers ___ As
pret - ty as ___ you please; But the bow that brid - ges

hea - ven And ov - er tops the trees, ___ And
builds a road from earth to sky _____ Is
pret - ti - er far _____ than these. ___

In the exercises in this section of the book it is advisable to write the melody on alternate staves, and to indicate either the complete chord scheme or the key changes and cadence chords on the stave below.

Exercise I. Write melodies to the following, indicating either the chord scheme, or the key changes and cadence chords :—

(a) Why so pale and wan, fond lover ?
      Prithee, why so pale ?
  Will, when looking well can't move her,
      Looking ill prevail ?
      Prithee, why so pale ?

                        (Suckling)

(b) My lute awake ! perform the last
      Labour that thou and I shall waste,
  And end that I have now begun ;
  For when this song is said and past,
      My lute, be still, for I have done.

                        (Wyatt)

(c) They went to sea in a sieve, they did,
      In a sieve they went to sea :
  In spite of all their friends could say,
  On a winter's morn, on a stormy day,
      In a sieve they went to sea !

                        (Lear)

(d) O it's I that am the captain of a tidy little ship,
  Of a ship that goes a-sailing on the pond ;

And my ship it keeps a-turning all around and all about;
But when I'm a little older, I shall find the secret out
How to send my vessel sailing on beyond.

(Stevenson)

Exercise II. Write melodies to the following :—

(a) Did you hear of the curate who mounted his mare,
And merrily trotted along to the fair !
Of creature more tractable none ever heard :
In the height of her speed she would stop at a word ;
But again with a word, when the curate said, ' Hey',
She put forth her mettle and galloped away.

(Peacock)

(b) He clasps the crag with crooked hands ;
Close to the sun in lonely lands,
Ringed with the azure world he stands.

The wrinkled sea beneath him crawls ;
He watches from his mountain walls,
And like a thunderbolt he falls.

(Tennyson)

(c) What was he doing, the great God Pan,
Down in the reeds by the river ?
Spreading ruin and scattering ban
Splashing and paddling with hoofs of a goat,
And breaking the golden lilies afloat
    With the dragon-fly on the river.

(E. B. Browning)

(d) Old Meg was brave as Margaret Queen
    And tall as Amazon ;
An old red blanket cloak she wore ;
    A chip hat had she on.
God rest her aged bones somewhere,
    She died full long agone.

(Keats)

2 Repetition of Words and Phrases

Read and work Part 3, Sections 5–7.

Words and phrases are occasionally repeated in a stanza
of verse. This gives one the opportunity to repeat or develop

figures already used, perhaps by means of sequence, and even on occasion to add further repetitions. See Ex. III (a) and (b).

It oftens happens, however, that although a poem does not repeat words, a musical setting will gain by doing so. Qualitative adjectives can be repeated, e.g., lovely, lovely rose ; verbs can be repeated, e.g., ' arise ' in Schubert's ' Hark, hark the lark', see Fig. 2 ; short phrases can be repeated, e.g., ' my lady sweet, arise ' in the same song. Notice also the repetition of ' tripping ' and of complete phrases, including the lingering cadence, in Fig. 3.

Fig. 2

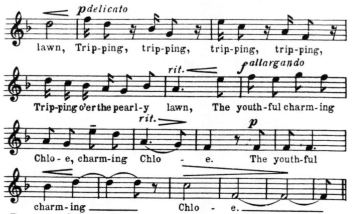

Beware of repeating incomplete sense, such as a noun at the end of a line. You will sometimes find this in a Gilbert and Sullivan opera and in nonsense jingles where the rhythm is all-important. But it is unsatisfactory in setting serious poetry to music.

There are times when the repetition of words seems necessary to produce a balanced length of phrase. See Ex. III (c) and (d). But at other times a repeated word or words will lengthen a phrase and produce irregularity. Ex. III (e) is a poem in which words or phrases could well be repeated, thus producing extended or additional phrases.

Then there are poems with a refrain which can be repeated ; others have nonsense words such as ' fol de rol ' or ' fa la la ' (Ex. III (f)) ; others again may imitate birds as in Ex. III (g).

Occasionally it may be possible to repeat words which came earlier in the stanza later in the setting, perhaps at the end, although they are not repeated in the poem. Be sure that the repetition is artistically justifiable and is not taking liberties with the poetry.

A study of songs by some of our best modern English composers will teach you a great deal with regard to the setting of words. The German lieder writers such as Schubert, Schumann and Brahms usually suffer in translation and are

therefore not such good models if studied in English.
' Hark, hark the lark ' quoted above is an exception, as the
original words were by an English poet, Shakespeare.

Exercise III. Write melodies to the following stanzas :—

(a) And wilt thou leave me thus !
    Say nay, say nay, for shame !
    —To save thee from the blame
    Of all my grief and grame.
    And wilt thou leave me thus ?
    Say nay ! say nay !

                   (Wyatt)

(b) The splendour falls on castle walls
      And snowy summits old in story :
    The long light shakes across the lakes
      And the wild cataract leaps in glory.
    Blow, bugle, blow, set the wild echoes flying,
    Blow, bugle ; answer, echoes, dying, dying, dying.
                   (Tennyson)

(c) Thy silver locks, once auburn bright,
    Are still more lovely in my sight
    Than golden beams of orient light,
            My Mary !

                   (Cowper)

(d) Love is a sickness full of woes,
      All remedies refusing ;
    A plant that with most cutting grows,
      Most barren with best using.
          Why so ?
    More we enjoy it, more it dies ;
    If not enjoyed, it sighing cries—
          Heigh ho !

                   (Daniel)

(e) Sweet in her green dell the flower of beauty slumbers,
      Lulled by the faint breezes sighing through her hair ;
    Sleeps she and hears not the melancholy numbers
      Breathed to my sad lute 'mid the lonely air.
                   (Darley)

(f)   John Cook he had a little grey mare,
    Hee ! haw ! hum !
  Her legs were long and her back was bare,
    Hee ! haw ! hum !
  John Cook went riding up Shooter's bank,
    Hee ! haw ! hum !
  The mare began to kick and prank.
    Hee ! haw ! hum !

(Old rhyme)

(g)   Spring, the sweet Spring, is the year's pleasant king ;
    Then blooms each thing, then maids dance in a ring,
  Cold doth not sting, the pretty birds do sing—
    Cuckoo, jug-jug, pu-we, to-witta-woo.

(Nashe)

(h)   'Tis a dull sight
    To see the year dying,
  When winter winds
    Set the yellow wood sighing :
      Sighing, O sighing !

(Fitzgerald)

3   Short Irregular Stanzas
Read and work Part 3, Section 8.

In working Section 2 you will have been getting some practice in phrase extension and contraction, so you will now be prepared for setting irregular stanzas.

Sometimes these seem to want irregular musical phrasing, but quite often they can with advantage be set to regular two-and four-bar phrases by repeating some word or phrase or by lengthening some word or syllable. Again, the study of good modern songs is the best means of acquiring discernment. The final result must seem natural and rhythmical whether the phrasing is regular or irregular.

Figs. 4, 5 and 6 show three different treatments of irregular stanzas. In Fig. 4 the musical setting is in regular four bar phrases, in Fig. 5 there is an extension towards the end, while in Fig. 6 the musical phrases as well as the metrical lines are all different and unusual lengths.

Fig. 4

Fig. 5

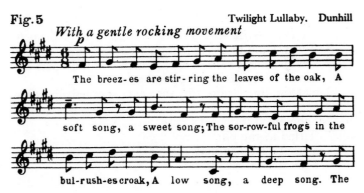

tin - kle is hushed in the rip - pling stream, The

mu - sic of twi-light says, "Hush thee and dream"__

__ And so the world sleeps. __

Fig. 6

Dreamily - as in a reverie   From a City Window. Parry

I hear the feet be-low   In the dark

street; They hur-ry and shuf-fle by, And go   on

er-rands bit-ter or sweet Whi-ther I can-not know.

Exercise IV. Write melodies to the following stanzas :—

(a) As I was going to Derby, all on a market day,
　　I met the finest ram, Sir, that ever was fed upon hay,
　　　Upon hay, upon hay, upon hay ;
　　I met the finest ram, Sir, that ever was fed upon hay.

(Anon)

(b) Magdalen at Michael's gate
　　　Tirled at the pin,
　　On Joseph's thorn sang the blackbird,
　　　' Let her in, let her in '.

(Henry Kingsley)

(c) ‘ I have no name ;
    I am but two days old ’.
    What shall I call thee ?
    ‘ I happy am,
    Joy is my name ’
    Sweet joy befall thee !

                                         (Blake)

(d) A pair of steady rooks
    Choose the safest of all nooks,
    In the hollow of a tree to build their home ;
      And while they kept within,
      They did not care a pin
    For any roving sportsman who might come.

                                    (E. Cook)

(e)   Go, lovely rose—
    Tell her that wastes her time and me,
      That now she knows,
    When I resemble her to thee,
    How sweet and fair she seems to be.

                                    (Waller)

(f) Love wing’d my hopes and taught me how to fly
    Far from base earth, but not to mount too high :
      For true pleasure
      Lives in measure,
      Which if men forsake,
    Blinded they into folly run and grief for pleasure take.

                                    (Anon)

4   The Eight Line Stanza or Poem
Read and work Part 3, Sections 10–13.

The easiest way to set eight lines of poetry is to consider them as two four-line verses and to let the second verse be more or less a repetition of the first, so that the song is really in strophic form. Simple ballad-like words are often suitable for this treatment. There are usually slight variants in the number of syllables in the corresponding lines, so it is as well to write out the second verse in full, making corresponding modifications in rhythm, so that the words flow naturally.

A rather more developed form is produced by modelling verse two on verse one but making considerable melodic alterations to suit the words. It may be that verse two can be given a climax that was lacking in verse one. Sometimes verse two will start differently, perhaps even in a different key, but soon return to the ideas and keys of verse one. Although the dominant key and relative major and minor keys are the most obvious keys in which to start verse two it is sometimes possible to be a little more venturesome, e.g., the major key a major third below the tonic key is often effective at this point.

In all the above arrangements the first four lines are meant to be more or less complete in themselves and end in the tonic key. But a more organic whole is produced if a continuous setting is used for the whole eight lines with the end of line four probably in the dominant or relative major or minor key. The difficulty lies in keeping the tune poised throughout, so that it does not feel it is coming to the end until line eight. One has to think of a suitable melodic and rhythmic setting for the words, of a modulation scheme, and of suitable places for repetition, development and contrast all at the same time. It is wise therefore to have had some preliminary practice in writing extended tunes containing several modulations before adding the complication of the words.

Read the words through several times, trying to feel their lilt. Decide before you start where you want to use repetition, development and contrast, and plan out a key scheme with this in mind. It is always possible to change your ideas later if you find the tune wants to go in a different way.

Instead of merely indicating the key changes and cadence chords you should occasionally add a complete piano accompaniment, perhaps with an introduction and a coda. The song will often be improved if it has a few bars of piano solo halfway through or even occasionally at other suitable places, and these interpolations could be sketched in even if you do not write a complete accompaniment.

There are plenty of examples by modern British song writers which can be studied as models for the setting of an eight line stanza or poem, as this is one of the most common forms of art song.

Exercise V. Write melodies to the following. Indicate the modulations and chief cadences or add a piano accompaniment.

(a)   Old Meg she was a gypsy,
            And lived upon the moors :
        Her bed it was the brown heath turf,
            And her house was out of doors.

        Her brothers were the craggy hills,
            Her sisters larchen trees—
        Alone with her great family
            She lived as she did please.

                                       (Keats)

(b)   Under the wide and starry sky
            Dig the grave and let me lie :
        Glad did I live and gladly die,
            And I laid me down with a will.

        This be the verse you grave for me:
            Here he lies where he long'd to be;
        Home is the sailor, home from sea,
            And the hunter home from the hill.

                                  (Stevenson)

(c)   My Peggy is a young thing,
            Just entered in her teens,
         Fair as the day, and sweet as May,
        Fair as the day, and always gay ;
            My Peggy is a young thing,
            And I'm not very auld,
         Yet well I like to meet her at
            The wawking* of the fauld.

                                  (Ramsay)

*Wawking = Watching

(d) My heart's in the highlands, my heart is not here,
　　　My heart's in the highlands a-chasing the deer ;
　　　Chasing the wild deer, and following the roe,
　　　My hearts in the highlands wherever I go.
　　　Farewell to the highlands, farewell to the North,
　　　The birthplace of valour, the country of worth ;
　　　Wherever I wander, wherever I rove,
　　　The hills of the highlands for ever I love.

(Burns)

(e) 　　　　The sun descending in the west,
　　　　　　　The evening star does shine ;
　　　　　The birds are silent in their nest,
　　　　　　　And I must seek for mine.
　　　　　The moon, like a flower,
　　　　　In heaven's high bower,
　　　　　With silent delight
　　　　　Sits and smiles on the night.

(Blake)

(f) 　　　　We are the music-makers,
　　　　　　　And we are the dreamers of dreams,
　　　　　Wandering by lone sea-breakers,
　　　　　　　And sitting by desolate streams ;
　　　　　World losers and world forsakers,
　　　　　　　On whom the pale moon gleams :
　　　　　Yet we are the movers and shakers
　　　　　　　Of the world for ever, it seems.

(O'Shaughnessy)

(g) 　　　　Haste thee nymph, and bring with thee
　　　　　Jest and youthful Jollity,
　　　　　Quips and Cranks, and wanton Wiles,
　　　　　Nods and Becks, and wreathed Smiles,
　　　　　Such as hang on Hebe's cheek,
　　　　　And love to live in dimple sleek ;
　　　　　Sport that wrincled Care derides,
　　　　　And Laughter holding both his sides.

(Milton)

5   The Twelve Line Stanza or Poem

Read and work Part 3, Sections 15 and 16.

Twelve line stanzas quite frequently have only two or three feet to a line, so they are no longer than a normal six line stanza, and they may be set very simply as a continuous whole, with few modulations. See Ex. VI (a) and (b).

A simple poem of three four line stanzas may be effectively set with each four lines to the same tune, making such slight modifications as may be necessary and perhaps changing the end of the third verse. See Ex. VI (c) and (d).

Other twelve line stanzas or poems clearly require a ternary form setting. But vary the last four lines as compared with the first four unless the style is very simple. See Ex. VI (e).

Yet other twelve line stanzas or poems change their style or mood or rhythm in the last four lines and therefore require a change of musical style too. A simple setting may be achieved by repeating the music of the first four lines for the second four and then breaking away for the last four. A more elaborate version may be produced by a ' durchcomponirt ' setting, in which every four lines is different, but unity is achieved by means of repetition and development of melodic figures and by the key scheme. The cadence at the end of line eight should usually be in the dominant or relative major or minor key, and the return to the tonic key at the ninth line will give unity of key even though a new musical idea is used. See Ex. VI (f) and (g).

Occasionally a twelve-line stanza may be found which does not divide up into sets of four lines. Study the meaning and the punctuation carefully and decide on a scheme which fits the words while still being satisfactory with regard to thematic development and modulation. See Ex. VI (h).

I

Space forbids the quotation of an example of each of these alternatives, but Fig. 7 shows a setting in ternary form with the ending modified. Study the modulations and the sequences and the effective word repetition at the end of the verse.

Fig. 7

Allegro giocoso   The Brook. Thiman

I come from haunts of coot and hern, I make a sud-den
sal - ly, And spar - kle out a - mong the fern, To
bick-er down a val - ley. By thir - ty hills I
hur-ry down, Or slip be-tween the rid - ges, By
twen-ty thorps, a lit - tle town And half a hun-dred
brid-ges. Till last by Phil - ip's
farm I flow To join the brim-ming riv - er, For
men may come and men may go, But I go on for
ev - er, for ev - er, for ev - er.

Exercise VI. Write melodies to the following. Indicate the modulations and chief cadences or add a piano accompaniment.

(a)
They stole little Bridget
    For seven years long ;
When she came down again
    Her friends were all gone.
They took her lightly back,
    Between the night and morrow,
They thought that she was fast asleep,
    But she was dead with sorrow.
They have kept her ever since
    Deep within the lake,
On a bed of flag leaves,
    Watching till she wake.

                       (Allingham)

(b)
O what a plague is love !
    How shall I bear it ?
She will inconstant prove,
    I greatly fear it.
She so torments my mind
That my strength faileth,
And wavers with the wind
    As a ship saileth.
Please her the best I may,
She loves still to gainsay ;
Alack and well a-day !
    Phillada flouts me.

                         (Anon.)

(c) Give a man a horse he can ride,
    Give a man a boat he can sail ;
And his rank and wealth, his strength and health,
    On sea nor shore shall fail.

Give a man a pipe he can smoke,
    Give a man a book he can read :
And his home is bright with a calm delight,
    Though the room be poor indeed.

Give a man a girl he can love
  As I, O my love, love thee ;
And his heart is great with the pulse of fate,
  At home, on land, on sea.

(James Thomson)

(d) Sister awake, close not your eyes,
    The day her light discloses ;
And the bright morning doth arise
    Out of her bed of roses.

See the dear sun, the world's bright eye
    In at our windows peeping ;
Lo ! how he blushes to espy
    Us idle wenches, sleeping.

Therefore awake, make haste, I say,
    And let us without staying,
All in our gowns of green so gay,
    Into the park a-maying.

(Anon.)

(e) Soldier, rest ! thy warfare o'er,
    Sleep the sleep that knows not breaking ;
Dream of battlefields no more,
    Days of danger, nights of waking.
In our Isle's enchanted hall,
    Hands unseen thy couch are strewing,
Fairy strains of music fall,
    Every sense in slumber dewing.
Soldier, rest ! thy warfare o'er,
    Dream of fighting fields no more :
Sleep the sleep that knows not breaking,
Morn of toil, nor night of waking.

(Scott)

(f) My Phillis hath the morning sun
    At first to look upon her ;
And Phillis hath morn-waking birds
    Her risings still to honour.
My Phillis hath prime feathered flowers,
    That smile when she treads on them ;

And Phillis hath a gallant flock,
   That leaps since she doth own them.
But Phillis hath too hard a heart,
   Alas that she should have it !
It yields no mercy to desert,
   Nor grace to those that crave it.

(Lodge)

(g) Good-bye, good-bye to summer !
     For Summer's nearly done ;
The garden smiling faintly,
     Cool breezes in the sun ;
Our thrushes now are silent,
     Our swallows flown away,—
But Robin's here, in coat of brown,
     And ruddy breast-knot gay.
       Robin, Robin Redbreast,
         O Robin dear !
       Robin singing sweetly
         In the falling of the year.

(Allingham)

(h) Hie away, hie away,
   Over bank and over brae,
Where the corpsewood is the greenest,
Where the fountains glisten sheenest,
Where the lady-fern grows strongest,
Where the morning dew lies longest,
Where the black-cock sweetest sips it,
Where the fairy latest trips it :
Hie to haunts right seldom seen,
Lovely, lonesome, cool and green,
Over bank and over brae
Hie away, hie away.

(Scott)

6   Long Irregular Stanzas or Poems

Read and work Part 3, Section 14.

When setting an irregular stanza to music, analyse it and think about it for a short while, noticing the number of feet in each line, where the words come to rest, and where you think there should be repetition, development or contrast.

Sometimes the irregularity is only apparent and the words can be set to regular phrases quite easily. See Ex. VII (a).

At other times there are obvious extensions, calling for sequences and other forms of thematic development. See Ex. VII (b).

Nonsense words give one a good deal of freedom, for they can be repeated to form regular phrases or used to form extensions. See Ex. VII (c).

Sometimes the repetition of a line or two may enhance or round off a stanza. This could be done in Ex. VII (d).

Some stanzas, however, are really very irregular and may require setting in a free, irregular rhythm. See Ex. VII (e) and (f).

Two songs which will repay careful study are ' If there were dreams to sell ' set by John Ireland and ' Five Eyes ' by Armstrong Gibbs, both published by Boosey & Hawkes. ' If there were dreams to sell ' consists of two stanzas, the first being ten lines and the second nine lines long. The setting contains a good deal of repetition and largely smooths out the rhythmic irregularities of the poem. ' Five Eyes ' consists of fourteen lines, but the setting repeats the first four lines at the end, thus making it into a sort of ternary form. Notice the seven bar phrase beginning with a descending chromatic scale at ' Squeaks from the flour sack,' and the corresponding seven bar phrase beginning with an ascending chromatic scale at ' then up he climbs',

Exercise VII. Write melodies to the following. Indicate the modulations and chief cadences or write a piano accompaniment.

(a) Fair daffodils, we weep to see
  You haste away so soon :
 As yet the early rising sun
  Has not attained his noon ;
   Stay, stay,
  Until the hasting day
   Has run
  But to the even-song ;
 And, having prayed together, we
  Will go with you along.   (Herrick)

(b)   Rats !
 They fought the dogs, and killed the cats,
  And bit the babies in the cradles,
 And ate the cheeses out of the vats,
  And licked the soup from the cook's own ladles,
 Split open the kegs of salted sprats,
 Made nests inside men's Sunday hats,
 And even spoiled the women's chats
  By drowning their speaking
  With shrieking and squeaking
 In fifty different sharps and flats. (Browning)

(c) Merrily swinging on briar and weed
  Near to the nest of his little dame,
 Over the mountain-side or the mead,
  Robert of Lincoln is telling his name :
   Bob-o'-link, bob-o'-link,
   Spink, spank, spink ;
 Snug and safe in that nest of ours,
 Hidden among the summer flowers,
   Chee, chee, chee.   (Bryant)

(d) Then sing, ye birds, sing, sing a joyous song !
  And let the young lambs bound
  As to the tabor's sound !
 We in thought will join your throng,

> Ye that pipe and ye that play,
> Ye that through your hearts to-day
> Feel the gladness of the May.

(Wordsworth)

(e)　Hey nonny no !
　　Men are fools that wish to die !
　　Is't not fine to dance and sing
　　When the bells of death do ring ?
　　Is't not fine to swim in wine,
　　And turn upon the toe
　　And sing hey nonny no !
　　When the winds blow and the seas flow ?
　　Hey nonny no !

(Anon.)

(f)　While that the sun with his beams hot
　　Scorched the fruits in vale and mountain,
　　Philon the shepherd, late forgot,
　　Sitting beside a crystal fountain
　　　In shadow of a green oak tree,
　　　Upon his pipe this song play'd he :
　　Adieu, Love, adieu, Love, untrue Love !
　　Untrue Love, untrue Love, adieu, Love !
　　Your mind is light, soon lost for new love.

(Anon.)

7　The Pentameter, Blank Verse and Prose

Pentameters are rarely set as songs, and they certainly present rhythmic difficulties. Sometimes the five feet can be contracted into four strong accents by putting two feet into the time of one. More often they are expanded into six, usually, but not always, by extending the last foot. This will probably result in three bar phrases and is perhaps the most common and natural method of setting pentameters. Occasionally they are expanded into eight and this is particularly likely to happen if some syllables or words call for expansion by means of long notes or melismas. The repetition of a word or words may have the same effect.

There is no need to follow the same method throughout

the stanza. One expects rhythmic variety in the setting of pentameters. Often the last line is extended.

Quite frequently the sense runs on from one line to the next and perhaps pauses in the middle of a line. This may actually be easier to set, as it may result in a regular four bar phrase. See Ex. VIII (c).

A pentameter line or two sometimes occurs in a stanza which is mainly in some other metre or in one with very mixed metres ; and a stanza which is mainly in pentameters may use other metres occasionally, to give variety and contrast. Both of these variants are easier to set than a complete stanza of pentameters. See Ex. VIII (c),

Study Fig. 8. The first three lines of verse are each compressed into four bars while the fourth line spreads out to seven. But the ear divides up the setting into two halves with the cadence of the first half at ' cypress trees,' i.e. half way through the third line, not at ' all the flowers,' as might have been expected. There is here a sort of double irregularity.

Fig. 8

I have been there before thee, O___ my love! Each wind-ing way I know___ and all the flowers, The sha-dow-y cy - press trees, the twi - light grove, Where rest, in fra - grant sleep,___ the en - chant - - ed hours.

Blank verse and prose are even more rarely set in song form, though they are often found in choral works. However, they are no more difficult to set than pentameters. Blank verse is, of course, pentameter rhythm without the rhyme, and poetic prose (the only kind one would want to set to music) naturally falls into phrases which are sometimes easier to set than a series of pentameters, even though they may vary considerably in length.

Exercise VIII. Write melodies to the following. Indicate the modulations and chief cadences or add a piano accompaniment.

(a)   My true love hath my heart, and I have his,
         By just exchange one for another given :
      I hold his dear, and mine he cannot miss,
         There never was a better bargain driven :
             My true love hath my heart, and I have his.

                                          (Sidney)

(b)   Wake now, my love, awake ! for it is time ;
      The Rosy thorne long since left Tithones bed,
      All ready to her silver coche to clyme ;
      And Phoebus gins to shew his·glorious hed.

                                          (Spenser)

(c)   There is sweet music here that softer falls
      Than petals from blown roses on the grass,
      Or night dews on still waters between walls
      Of shadowy granite, in a gleaming pass ;
      Music that gentler on the spirit lies,
      Than tired eyelids upon tired eyes ;
      Music that brings sweet sleep down from the blissful
         skies.
      Here are cool mosses deep,
      And thro' the moss the ivies creep,
      And in the stream the long leaved flowers weep,
      And from the craggy ledge the poppy hangs in sleep.

                                          (Tennyson)

(d)   How sweet the moonlight sleeps upon this bank !
      Here will we sit, and let the sounds of music
      Creep in our ears ; soft stillness and the night

Become the touches of sweet harmony.
Sit Jessica. Look how the floor of heaven
Is thick inlaid with patines of bright gold :
There's not the smallest orb which thou behold'st
But in his motion like an angel sings,
Still quiring to the young eyed cherubins ;
Such harmony is in immortal souls ;
But whilst this muddy vesture of decay
Doth grossly close it in, we cannot hear it.

(Shakespeare)

N.B. Vaughan Williams omits the words 'Sit Jessica' in his setting of these words in ' Serenade to Music ' and you may prefer to do the same.

(e) Hark to the tumult of many peoples !
They make a noise, like the noise of the seas !
Hark to the roar of nations !
They make a roar, like the roaring of mighty waters.
The nations shall roar like the roaring of many waters,
But God shall rebuke them. And they shall flee afar off ;
They shall be chased, as the chaff of the mountains
before the wind,
And like rolling dust before the whirlwind.

(Isaiah)

(f) Any of the psalms of David.

PART V

MELODY ANALYSIS

1 Adding Phrase Marks To Melodies—Regular Phrase Structure

Before adding phrase marks to an unphrased melody number the bars, starting with the first complete bar. If they add up to a multiple of four the tune is probably regular.

When analysing a melody the first essential is to hear the tune accurately, and it should be possible to do this without resorting to a piano or other instrument. Singing aloud is a help but eventually it should be possible to hear melodies entirely mentally. If mental hearing is found difficult, constant practice may be necessary, making use of solfa and time names and stopping at a difficult interval until you are sure you have heard it accurately. Be sure that you start on the right note of the scale, as otherwise the tune will be heard quite wrongly. Never lose the feel of the tonic even if the tune modulates—sing the tonic occasionally in the middle of the tune to be sure the relationships are right. Do not start to analyse until you have heard or sung the tune correctly.

Sing through Fig. 1 in this way.

Fig. 1

Notice the beat of the bar on which the tune begins. The simplest tunes will start every phrase in the same part of the bar : e.g. if a tune in ¾ time begins on the third beat you can expect the first phrase to end on the second beat of bar 4 and the second phrase to start on the third beat of the same bar. This is a special feature of dance tunes : e.g. a gavotte starts every phrase on the third crotchet in ⁴₄ time, while the bourrée, also in ⁴₄ time, starts on the fourth crotchet. Even in other kinds of music this is so likely to happen that it is sensible to see if it does so before considering other alternatives. And, where a change of rhythmic shape does occur, there will still usually be the same number of strong beats in each phrase, thus making it four bars or two bars long.

Expect the phrase ends to occur every four bars, in the appropriate part of the bar. Look therefore to see if you can hear cadences at these places and put a comma above and between the notes thus ' where you think each phrase comes to an end. The repetition or development of a previous phrase often helps one to see the beginning of a phrase, though sometimes a phrase which begins on the first beat of the bar returns later with an anacrusis added, and vice versa.

Beware of thinking that a long note always denotes the end of a phrase. It can occur at the beginning or in the middle, and a feminine ending in ⁴₄ time may finish with

♩ ♩ . The harmony at such a cadence is really the

deciding factor, for the tune will finally come to rest on a note of the last chord.

In Fig. 1 the first phrase ends with an imperfect cadence in bar 4. The D is part of the dominant chord whereas the E is not. We therefore expect the phrase to end with the D, particularly as this is where it is rhythmically due to end. When we notice that this means that the second phrase not only starts on the fourth beat, as did the first, but starts with the same tune, we are left in no doubt that the D marks the end of the phrase.

Now look at bar 8. We notice that the melody has

modulated and therefore we expect a perfect cadence in key G. [♪ score] is another feminine ending, and the new phrase starts on the fourth beat as before.

But now look at bar twelve [♪ score] does not look so much like a feminine ending, for such endings fall by step much more frequently than they rise by leap. When we see that [♪ score] is repeated sequentially in the next next bar, we realise that there must be a change of rhythm, and that the new phrase starts on the third beat instead of the fourth.

Now put in commas to mark the end of each phrase in Fig. 1.

Next, consider whether any of these phrases break up into smaller sections. They may break into sections exactly half way, or into units at quarter distances. The presence of repeated rhythmic figures or of sequences usually denotes the breaking up of a phrase. On the other hand a phrase which is flowing onwards just at the place where it might break up is probably unbroken. Look, therefore, at the possible breaking-up places. Sing the phrase broken and unbroken to see which feels natural and musical.

Now mark any subdivisions in Fig. 1 by adding phrase marks and after doing so compare your version with Fig. 2. Be sure to draw your phrase marks accurately : they must always begin and end exactly over the right note, never in between notes or at a bar line.

Fig. 2

Melodies with a large number of notes to the bar often consist of two bar phrases. Sections will then be one bar long and units only half a bar, and even shorter figures may occur.

Sometimes more than one way of phrasing a melody is possible. This might happen with Fig. 13. After phrasing it yourself compare the phrasing with the original if you can hear a performance or procure a copy.

Do not take for granted that the phrase marks are correctly shown in all printed music you may meet. Some editions print phrase marks as if they were artistic decorations without any musical significance ! Judge for yourself how accurate they are.

Exercise I. Add phrase marks to the following melodies, showing any subdivisions of phrases that may occur and indicating the main cadences by means of a comma.

a)
Fig. 3

b)

Fig. 4

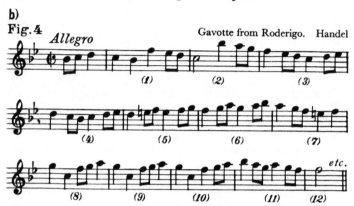

Gavotte from Roderigo.　Handel

c)

Fig. 5

Serenade Op. 22.　Beethoven

N.B.—In the above the first phrase ends in bar 4, but on which note? Sing it ending on each one in turn, in order to see which sounds the most natural and which way makes the best start for the new phrase. What cadence is probably implied and does the B or the A belong to the last chord of this cadence? You may change your mind after singing through the entire tune.

d)
Fig. 6

e)
Fig. 7

K

N.B.—Bar 4 should be phrased thus :

If the notes had been  the

phrase would have had to continue on to the last quaver,
so as to come to rest on a note of the dominant chord.

f)
Fig.8

Bourree from Water Music.   Handel

Two Part Invention No. 1.   Bach

g)
Fig.9

Moderato

h)
Fig. 10   Pastorale. Scarlatti

i)
Fig. 11   Sarabande. Couperin

j)
Fig. 12   Estrella from Carnaval. Schumann

Fig. 13 *Allegretto* Symphony No. 3. Brahms

Further suitable exercises may be found in the following works by Schumann :—

Album for the Young, Nos. 5, 19, 25 and 27 ;

Kinderscenen No. 2 ; and Slumber Song.

2   Adding Phrase Marks to Melodies—Irregular Phrase Structure

Read Part 3, Sections 4–8, in order to become familiar with various forms of phrase irregularity.

Number the bars, starting with the first complete bar. If the melody is (e.g.) fifteen or seventeen bars long there must be irregularity somewhere. But even a sixteen bar melody may be irregular, it may have (e.g.) a three bar followed by a five bar phrase.

Occasionally, irregular melodies consist of a series of phrases all the same length such as 5+5+5 bars. But more often a tune starts by being regular, and irregularity comes later when the pattern is set and the listener is ready to appreciate the extension or contraction of a phrase.

Look out also for examples of cadence repetition or extension at the end of a melody. See Fig. 55 for an example of a long note at the end of a melody turning a four bar phrase into a five.

Notice any repetitions, sequences or developments, for they help one to recognise the beginning of a new phrase or section. And analyse the phrase ends to be sure you can hear cadences there.

Sometimes phrases overlap, the first note or two of one phrase coinciding with the last note or two of the previous phrase. See Fig. 14, where the F♯ in bar 8 marks the cadence of the previous phrase but is also the first note of a repetition of bar 1 in a new key.

Fig. 14   Album for the Young No. 31.   Schumann

Sing through, analyse and phrase Fig. 15, then compare your conclusions with those given below.

Fig. 15

At first sight this seems to be a regular melody, as it is sixteen bars long. But there is no doubt that a perfect cadence in the dominant key occurs at bar seven. Where is the first cadence, in bar three or bar four? In spite of the fact that it is

usual to start with a four bar phrase, 3^3 marks the end of the
first phrase. This conclusion is reached by comparing
1—3^3 with 13^1—16^4 and by noticing the sequences in
3^4—4^3 and 4^4—5^3, which belong to the same phrase. The
fact that 7^4 starts with the same figure as 3^4 is an additional
reason for feeling that 3^4 is the beginning of a phrase.

13^1 is clearly the beginning of the last phrase, as it returns
to the opening idea and is preceded by an imperfect cadence.
Therefore the phrase before this must be five bars long. What
has caused the extension? The phrase breaks up thus:
7^4—8^3, 8^4—9^3, 9^4—10^3 10^4—11^3 and 11^3—12^4. 10^4—11^3
seems to be an interpolation, for the phrase would sound
quite regular without it.

Finally, notice that bars 15 and 16 augment the final
cadence, as compared with bar 3.

Before starting to work Ex. II, study Fig. 37 which consists
of two fourteen-bar phrases, and notice the clever use of
phrase extension and sequence.

Exercise II. Add phrase marks to the following melodies,
showing any subdivisions of phrases that may occur, and
indicating the main cadences by means of a comma. State
where irregular phrases occur, and comment upon how the
irregularity has been caused, if there is an obvious reason.

a)
Fig. 16

Allegro non troppo   Finale from Symphony No. 1.   Brahms

b)
Fig. 17
Allegro vivace   Morning Song.   Mendelssohn

c)
Fig. 18   Gavotte from Organ Concerto No. 11.   Handel
Allegro moderato

d)
Fig. 19   Full Fathom Five.   Johnson
Moderato

e)
Fig. 20

German Folk Tune

f)
Fig. 21

Allegro

Finale from Symphony No. 2.   Brahms

g)
Fig. 22

A major

Ibid

h)

Fig. 23

i)

Fig. 24

j)

Fig. 25

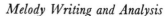

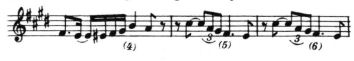

Further suitable exercises are the following :—
(1) Song of the Willow (Traditional).
(2) Nymphs and Shepherds (Purcell).
(3) Chorus of Virgins from Samson (Handel).
(4) Under the Greenwood Tree (Arne).
(5) Theme of St. Antony Variations (Brahms).

3 The Recognition of Key

Read Part 3, Sections 1 and 2 and 10–16.

It is helpful to realise what modulations are likely to
take place in a given tune, so begin by making a list of all
the related keys to the key centre of the melody. Other
modulations may occur, particularly in the work of modern
composers, but those to related keys are much more common.
An elaborate modulation scheme would require harmony as
well as melody for its proper recognition. Even with a simple
scheme it is often possible to harmonise a tune in more than
one key in some places. You have only to study some of the
chorales which Bach has harmonised in alternative ways to
realise this.

It is helpful also, to remember that modulation to the
sharp side of the tonic more often occurs near the beginning
of a tune, and modulation to the flat side nearer the end.

Sing through the tune carefully and accurately. It is probable that, after doing this, you will already be sure of several if not all of the modulations, but the knowledge will require checking in the ways shown below.

Next, phrase the melody in the way shown in Sections 1 and 2. Modulation is very much linked up with phrase shape and you have much more chance of recognising key changes correctly if you have analysed the rhythmic and melodic structure. For example, a sequence often indicates a change of key, and a phrase repeated later in a tune at a different pitch is probably in a different key.

The correct recognition of modulation depends primarily upon a good aural sense, for you should always be able to sing the new tonic when a tune has modulated. It can, however, be checked by seeing if the notes imply a cadence in the new key. Even when a short transition occurs in the middle of a phrase it is usually possible to hear dominant and tonic harmony underneath the melody.

The other method of checking your aural instinct is to look at the accidentals. Add the accidentals in the given phrase to those in the key signature in order to find the probable key. The presence of one accidental much sharper than the others probably indicates the leading note of a minor key. Remember that accidentals denoting the two forms of the melodic minor scale may contradict each other. E.g. in D minor there may be B♭ and B♮, C and C♯. Remember also that in modulating from a minor key to its relative major, there are no accidentals at all.

Look at the following phrase endings of a melody in D major.

Fig. 26

(*a*) probably indicates a modulation to A major ; (*b*) shows the melodic form of B minor. Do not make the mistake of saying it is B major. This is most unlikely, as B major is not a related key, whereas B minor is the relative minor ; (*c*) contradicts the C♯ in the signature and is probably a modulation to G major, though it may be E minor. The context will probably make one appear more likely than the other but sometimes it is impossible to tell if the harmonies are not given ; (*d*) must be in a minor key, for no major key has G♮ and D♯ in its scale. The sharpest note, D♯ will probably be the leading note. The presence of a diminished fifth or augmented fourth often indicates the presence of the leading note. See (*e*).

An implied modulation may be more difficult to recognise. A descending scale-wise melody at a cadence often leads to a new tonic. In a tune in D major a phrase ending as at Fig. 27 (*a*) probably indicates a modulation to A major, while (*b*) probably indicates a modulation to B minor.

Fig. 27

A chromatic note does not always indicate modulation, however. It may only be a decorating note, such as a chromatic passing note or a lower auxiliary note, approached and quitted by step. A chromatically altered note which is approached by leap is more likely to imply modulation, though if it is quitted by step it may even then be an appoggiatura in the original key. A chromatic note approached and quitted by leap is sure to be an essential note and to imply a change of key. Your ear is the final arbiter, but a knowledge of whether the suggested modulation is likely to occur at this particular place will help. For example, in Fig. 17, the F♯ in bars 1 and 2 is hardly likely to imply a modulation so near the beginning of the melody and it could be a chromatic passing note. But the F♯ in bar 6 is quitted by leap, and the cadence at bar 8 leaves one in no doubt that the music has modulated to the dominant key half-way through, as might have been expected. The G♯ in bar 2 is also a chromatic passing note.

Name the key at the point at which it is established, not at the first hint of a change. As a check, go to the piano after you have named the keys and play a perfect cadence after the phrase or section which you consider to have modulated, to see if it sounds right.

Exercise III. Phrase the following melodies. Then, by reference to bar numbers, name the key changes in each melody. All the extracts begin and end in the same key.

(a) Fig. 8.
(b) Fig. 11.

c)
Fig. 28

Allegro

Ode to Joy. Schubert

d)
Fig. 29

Moderato

German Folk Tune

e)
Fig.30

Allegro   Bourrée. Handel

f)
Fig. 31

Andante   Sarabande. Purcell

g)
Fig. 32

Gavotte. Bach

h)
Fig. 33

Hornpipe from the Water Music. Handel

i)
Fig. 34

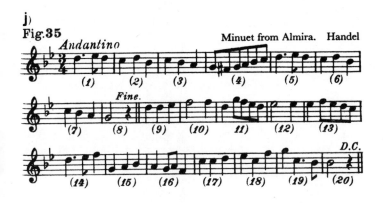

j)
Fig.35

Andantino   Minuet from Almira.   Handel

k)
Fig.36

Allegro moderato   Bourrée.   Bach

4 Thematic Development

Before answering questions on thematic development, hear the melody right through and add the phrase marks, even though you are only being asked about one particular part of it. You cannot deal with one part without having a conception of the whole.

Themes may be developed in many ways. They may be reproduced in exact or modified sequence. But remember that the word ' sequence ' may only be used if the phrase follows on immediately. If some other phrase intervenes then we can only say that it is repeated a third higher or fourth lower, as the case may be. If this repetition involves a change of key state the new key.

The melody may be decorated ; or the intervals may be changed, larger leaps perhaps leading towards a climax ; or the whole or part of the phrase may proceed by inverse motion, as so often happens in Bach.

There may also be rhythmic changes . some note or notes may be longer or shorter than before ; the rhythm of the phrase may be expanded or contracted ; or the whole phrase may be shown in augmentation or diminution.

Part of a phrase may be developed. A good method of leading up to a climax is to repeat the quicker half of a figure twice over, and perhaps go on to repeat a quarter of the figure four times over. The contraction of rhythmic unit that thus occurs heightens the tension most effectively.

Fig. 37 is a fine example of rhythmic development, leading upwards to a series of climaxes and producing long

phrases. The germ of the 27 bars is ♩♩|♩ , which comes in
(*b*) and (*d*). Long notes are added to make it a longer section,
only to be taken off again as the figure works up. Notice
how, from bars 7-12, the quicker half of ♩♩|♩ ♩♩
is used thus : ♩♩|♩ , and then is brought down to a
quarter ♩♩|♩ ; and how later the quicker half of (*d*) is
used in the same way. Notice also the overlapping of phrases
in many places, and particularly half-way through at bar 14.
The whole passage repays careful analysis.

Fig. 37

Mastersingers Overture. Wagner

Fig. 38 shows note lengths contracted and producing a very similar effect. ♩. ♪│♪♩. │ becomes ♫♫ │ and then ♫♫

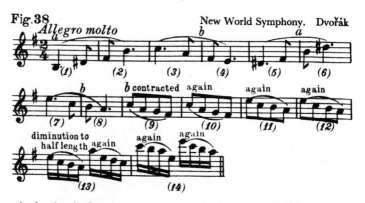

Fig.38

Allegro molto   New World Symphony. Dvořák

A rhythmic figure can have its pitch changed considerably and still be a recognisable development of the original. But the same melodic line with a change of rhythmic shape and accent (apart from diminution as shown above) has much less resemblance. We are more conscious of rhythmic similarities than of pitch ones. That is why composers such as Beethoven and Brahms develop their rhythmic subjects much more than their melodic ones.

When commenting upon thematic development always refer to a phrase or section or unit or figure, not to isolated notes, or even several notes together unless they do form a rhythmic group. Do not comment bar by bar unless the bar happens to be a rhythmic unit—nothing gives away one's lack of musicianship more! It is useful to refer to parts of a bar thus : 4^3 represents the third beat of the fourth bar.

State the facts as concisely and accurately as possible, without being too 'wordy'. Get to the essential point, trying to summarise differences between one phrase and another. Use such words as 'modified sequence', 'decoration', 'figure rising', 'note values changed', 'augmentation', 'key changed to dominant', and do not go into differences note by note. If there are many slight changes that cannot easily be summarised, say that the figure is 'developed'.

Exercise IV. Phrase the following melodies, and then answer the questions given below about each one :—

(a) Fig. 6. Comment on the use made of the opening figure each time it recurs throughout the piece.

(b) Fig. 13. Comment on the use made of the first six notes throughout the piece.

(c) Fig. 18. Comment on the use made of the opening figure each time it recurs throughout the piece.

(d) Fig. 25. Label each phrase, e.g. (a) (b) (a^d). etc.

(e) Fig. 28. Compare bars 5-8 with 13-16.

(f) Fig. 30. (1) What use is made of the figure ending at 2^3? (2) What use is made of 4^4—6^3? (3) Point out a sequence in the second half which might change key.

(g) Fig. 34. Compare the first section, ending at 8^2 with 20^3—28^2, accounting for any similarities or differences.

h)
Fig. 39

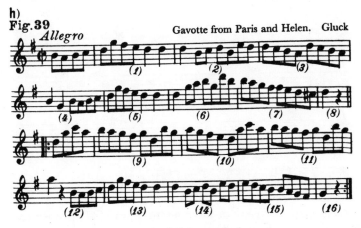

Gavotte from Paris and Helen.   Gluck

Compare the endings of the two halves.

i)

Fig. 40

The opening figure is used four times. Comment upon its use at each repetition,

j)

Fig. 41

Compare 2³—4² with the opening phrase. Point out two sequences and a modified sequence.

k)
Fig. 42

Two Part Invention No. 9.   Bach

Compare bars 1-4 with 9-12 and 12-17.

l)
Fig. 43

Overture to Hercules.   Handel

By reference to bar and beat numbers point out one sequence, two modified sequences and one example of phrase modification.

m)

Fig. 44

Allegro molto e vivace   Minuet from Symphony No. 1.   Beethoven

C minor   *(1)*   *(2)*   *(3)* E♭ major *(4)*   *(5)*   *(6)*

(7) C minor *(8)*   *(9)* A♭ major *(10)*   *(11)*   *(12)*

D♭ major   *(13)*   *(14)*   *(15)*   *(16)*   *(17)*

Comment on the use made of the first 4 bars.

n)

Fig. 45   2nd Movement from Symphony No. 3.   Brahms

Andante   a   b   c

(1)   *(2)*   *(3)*   *(4)*

(5)   *(6)*   *(7)*   *(8)*

(9)   *(10)*   *(11)*   *(12)*   *(13)*

(14)   *(15)*   *(16)*   *(17)*   *(18)*

(19)   *(20)*   *(21)*   *(22)*

Give a detailed continuous commentary on this extract, showing the development of the figures (*a*), (*b*) and (*c*).

o)
Fig. 46

Comment upon any thematic development found in this extract.

p)
Fig. 47

Describe the thematic development throughout this extract.

Further suitable examples on which similar questions may be asked will be found in Schumann's Album for the Young, Nos. 1, 3, 13 and 17.

5   Complete Analysis

If you are required to write a detailed analysis of a melody it is wise to tabulate it, as this clarifies your own mind as well as making your meaning clearer to the reader.

Phrase the melody first, noting any irregular phrase lengths.   Mark the key changes and any repetitions, sequences or other forms of development.

From this, write out an analysis, phrase by phrase, commenting upon the material used, the keys to which modulation is made and any irregularities of structure.

Analyse Fig. 48 and then compare your analysis with that shown below.

Fig. 48

Bourrée from 3rd Orchestral Suite.   Bach

Anacrusis-4^3	Opening phrase in D major. The figure marked (*a*) is repeated immediately, descending a third lower and is much used throughout the piece. The phrase runs straight on to
$4^{3\frac{1}{2}}$—8^3	Answering phrase, modulating from D major to A major. The (*a*) figure is used twice more, rising each time. This section is repeated.
8^4—12^3	The first two bars are the same as the opening phrase but in A major. The phrase then modulates back to D major.
$12^{3\frac{1}{2}}$—16^3	A new rhythmic figure appears ♪ | ♫ ♩ , and is used four times in E minor.
16^4—20^3	The rhythm of the opening phrase is ·used. The phrase ends in B minor.
20^4—24^3	The (*a*) figure is used again twice, with varying intervals. The phrase returns to the tonic, but immediately modulates to G major. It runs straight on to
$24^{3\frac{1}{2}}$—28^3	$25^{3\frac{1}{2}}$—26^3 is a sequence of $24^{3\frac{1}{2}}$—25^3. The phrase modulates from D major to A major and runs straight on to
$28^{3\frac{1}{2}}$—32^3	The final phrase is in D major. $28^{3\frac{1}{2}}$—30^3 corresponds to $12^{3\frac{1}{2}}$—16^3 in rhythm. Bars 8^4—32^3 are then repeated.

Exercise V. Phrase and analyse the following melodies :
(a) Fig. 3.   (b) Fig. 7.   (c) Fig. 16.   (d) Fig. 31.
(e) Fig. 32.   (f) Fig. 33.

g)
Fig. 49

h)
Fig. 50

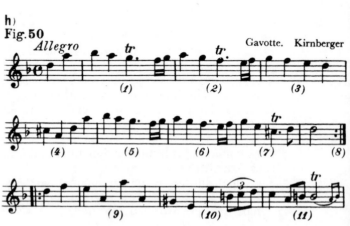

i)
Fig. 51 *Moderato*   Blow, blow, thou winter wind.   Arne

j)
Fig. 52

Air from Time and Truth.   Handel

l)

Fig.54

m)

Fig.55

6 Questions on Phrasing and Analysis

Exercise VI.

a)
Fig.56

Air from the Peasant Cantata. Bach

(1) Add the phrase marks.
(2) Compare bars 10-13 with 1-5.
(3) Compare bars 14-17 with 6-9.
(4) Point out an example of sequence.

b)
Fig.57

Minuet. Rameau

(1) Add phrase marks.

(2) Comment on bars 9-12.

(3) On what previous material is bars 13-16 based, and how is it used?

(4) Comment on bars 17-20.

(5) Compare bars 13 and 21.

---

c)
Fig.58

Old German Folk Tune

M

(1) Add phrase marks.

(2) By reference to bar numbers name the keys throughout the tune.

(3) On what previously heard material is bars 4³—8² based, and how is it used?

(4) Point out an example of a modified sequence.

(5) Compare bars 12³—16² and 16³—20² with the opening phrase.

---

d)
Fig. 59

Andante   Air from Theodora. Handel

(1) Add phrase marks.

(2) Comment on any unusual phrase lengths.

(3) In what keys is the music at (a) bar 15 ; (b) bars 22-23; (c) bars 24-25 ; (d) bar 29?

(4) Compare bars 1-6, 17-21 and 26-29.

(5) Point out an example of a modulatory sequence.

Fig.60

Bourrée from 5th French Suite. Bach

(1) Add phrase marks.

(2) Comment on the length of the first half, and compare it with the length of the second half.

(3) Comment on the uses made of the first three notes.

(4) Point out three examples of inversion.

(5) In what keys is the music at bars 10, 18 and 22 ?

f)
Fig.61

Scherzo from String Quartet. Haydn

(1) Add phrase marks.

(2) How do you account for the first section being ten bars long?

(3) State the keys passed through in bars 10^3—20^2, and comment on the thematic development in these bars.

---

g)
Fig.62

Violin Concerto. Mendelssohn

(1) Add phrase marks.

(2) Bars 20⁴—29² are an example of phrase extension. Comment on how the extension has been made.

(3) In what two keys might Mendelssohn have harmonised bars 8²—12¹? Do you know which key he actually used?

(4) Comment on the thematic development in the first twelve bars.

h)
Fig. 63   Last movement of Symphony No. 1.   Brahms
Allegro

(1) Add phrase marks.

(2) By reference to bar numbers show in detail how the whole of this tune grows from one idea.

i)
Fig. 64   Third movement of Symphony No. 2.   Brahms

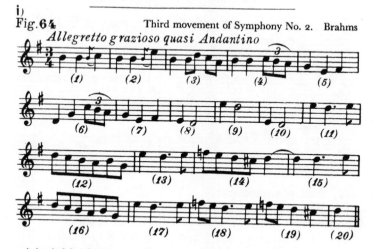

(1) Add phrase marks.

(2) In what key does the passage end ?

(3) Comment on the first phrase (bars 1-4).

(4) Comment on bar 8, and the uses made of it later.

(5) Compare bars 15-20 with 11-14.

Similar questions may be set on the following :—

   (a) 'If with all your hearts' (Mendelssohn). Contains extension and coda.

   (b) 'O rest in the Lord' (Mendelssohn). Contains cadential augmentation.

   (c) 'When daisies pied' (Arne). Contains phrase extension.

   (d) Minuet from London Symphony (Haydn). Contains extensions.

   (e) Slow movement from Symphony No. 5 (Beethoven). 8 bars extended to 22.

PART VI

ANALYSIS OF SHORT PIANO PIECES

Part 5, Melody Analysis, should have been worked through before attempting Part 6.

In some ways, analysis of a complete piano piece is easier than that of a melody. The harmonies often help to show the phrasing, and cadences and modulation can more easily be recognised. It does, however, demand a higher standard of mental hearing. Constant practice is needed by the average student in order to develop this faculty.

1 Melody

Melody analysis has already been dealt with. Look out for sequences and other forms of development, such as inverse movement, the return of a melodic phrase in a different key, and so on.

2 Counterpoint

(a) *Part Writing.* An understanding of the notation of contrapuntal writing is necessary. We speak of ' voices ' even if contrapuntal music is written for strings or piano ; and where there are two voice parts on the same stave the higher voice will have its stems up and the lower voice its stems down, even though the parts cross.

Sometimes, in piano writing, a voice part moves from one stave to another, for ease in performance. Follow the line of the middle voice part in Fig. 1.

Fig. 1   Fugue 7 of " the 48 ". Bach

Play through each voice part in a three or four part fugue, in order to get practice in part reading.

Students are apt to forget the presence of a long note when other parts have moved on, yet it is an essential part of the texture, and must be taken into account in naming chords and cadences. Play all the notes that are sounding at each half bar in Fig. 1 above.

(b) *Imitation.* When one voice part copies another, immediately afterwards, at the same or a different pitch, the parts are said to be in imitation. See beginning of Fig. 8. The imitation need not be exact, and it may be by inversion. It must occur in *different* voice parts; if it were in the same voice part it would be 'sequence'.

(c) *Canon.* When imitation is exact, and continues for some time, it is said to form a canon. A canon is frequently at the unison or octave, but it may occur at other intervals' distance, and it, also, may be by inversion.

(d) *Fugato.* A fugue is a highly involved contrapuntal composition which begins with all the voices entering separately, and imitating each other in tonic and dominant keys alternately. If imitative entries occur in this way in a work which is not a fugue they are sometimes called 'fugal entries' or 'fugato'.

(e) *Invertible Counterpoint.* When two voice parts reappear with the upper part at the bottom and the lower part at the top they are said to be in invertible or double counterpoint. This frequently occurs in a fugue, but it can be found elsewhere, even in harmonic forms such as a Beethoven sonata. The second half of a binary form dance movement in a suite sometimes begins with the opening bars in invertible counterpoint in the dominant.

Fig. 2

1st half

Bourrée from 6th French Suite. Bach
2nd half

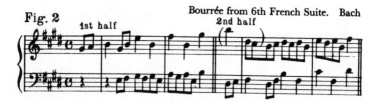

(f) *Triple Counterpoint*.   Sometimes three parts are in invertible counterpoint, and the music is then said to be in triple counterpoint.

(g) *Pedal*.   When one note is held or repeated for some time against changing harmonies it is said to form a pedal. It is frequently in the bass, but it can occur in upper parts and then it is termed an inverted pedal.   Usually the held note is the tonic or the dominant of the key and sometimes it appears in a decorated form.   The beginning of Fig. 7 shows a simple example in which the pedal note is always part of the chord.   Some authorities confine the use of the word 'pedal' to passages where the held note is not always part of the harmony.   See Fig. 11, bars 8-12.   Pedals can last for several pages, and modulations can occur over them. A dominant pedal is an effective means of creating a desire for the return of the tonic key, as, for example, at the end of the development section in sonata form ; and a tonic pedal frequently occurs at the end of a piece.

3   Harmony

(a) *Chords*.   It is assumed that the student has some knowledge of harmony.   Triads in root position ($^5_3$ from bass), first inversion ($^6_3$ from bass), and second inversion ($^6_4$ from bass) are easily recognised.   Chords of the 7th, 9th, 11th and 13th consist of a series of thirds (though some of the notes may be omitted).   When these discords are inverted the best method of finding the root is to add thirds below the lowest note until the chord consists of a series of thirds, and is therefore in root position.

Fig. 3 shows two inverted chords which are brought down in this way.   (*a*) is thereby proved to be the last inversion of the supertonic 7th, and (*b*) is the third inversion of the dominant 13th.   The dominant is frequently the root of these higher discords.

Fig. 3

Diminished 7ths should also be known, as they are frequently used for modulation purposes. By dropping each of the notes down a semitone in turn and enharmonically changing the names, four different dominant 7ths can be produced, each of which can be resolved in a major or minor key. Therefore, a diminished 7th can resolve into eight different keys !

Fig. 4

As one does not know which way they will move they are sometimes deliberately used to produce a vague tonality. A prolonged diminished 7th or a series of them (for one can resolve on another) can produce a sort of no-man's-land between one key and another. Look at the first movement of Beethoven's Sonata, Op. 2, No. 3. There you will find eight bars of diminished 7ths just before the cadenza.

(b) *Essential and Unessential Notes.* Before harmonic analysis of anything more than the simplest passage can be attempted the student should be able to differentiate between essential and unessential notes. He should be able to recognise the most common types of unessential notes (passing notes, auxiliary notes, suspensions and anticipations). Long notes and notes that leap are usually essential notes. In bars 1-4 of Fig. 6 all the unessential notes are bracketed. Analyse the chords throughout this example.

The most elaborate and chromatic texture may be a decorated version of a simple diatonic chord, particularly in the piano pieces of such composers as Chopin and Liszt. The student who can grasp the underlying harmony at once has a great advantage as a sight reader.

(c) *Cadences and Phrasing.* Expect a phrase to last four bars and look to see if you can recognise a cadence at this point. The subject has been dealt with in the melody writing and melody analysis parts of this book and cadences are easier to recognise harmonically than melodically. Be prepared, of course, for changes of key. Look at the cadences in Fig. 6

at bars 3-4, 13-14, 33-34 and 41-42. Then name the cadences in Fig. 11, bars 3-4, 7-8, 15-16, 23-24, 27-28 and 40-43.

4 Modulation

There is little new to add to what has been written in the melodic sections of this book. Make a list of the related keys to the main key of the piece, and expect these keys to occur. Remember that accidentals that move by step may only be decorations such as lower auxiliary notes, and may therefore not cause a change of key.

Try to hear the music mentally and to sing the tonic at each cadence or whenever you suspect a change of key. A key is usually established by dominant and tonic chords, which you should be able to recognise.

5 Analysis of Form

Short extracts and pieces of the sort dealt with here will not make use of the longer and more elaborate forms. Do not expect every piece to be in one of the regular forms such as binary or ternary. Many pieces cannot be given a label in this way, yet their form is perfectly clear and recognisable.

6 Complete Analysis

If you are required to analyse an extract or piece try to hear it through first, then annotate the copy, marking the changes of key, any repetitions or developments, any contrapuntal devices used, etc. Then tabulate it phrase by phrase.

Try to hear Fig. 5 or play it through on the piano. Notice the comments written over the music, then go carefully through the analysis given below.

Fig. 5 *Allegro* Prelude 20 of " the 48 ". Bach

Analysis of Fig. 5.

1-4	Opening phrase in A minor. R.H. Fig. (*a*) in bar 1, repeated twice in rising modified sequences in bars 2 and 3. L.H. uses a decorated tonic pedal (*b*).
5-8	Answering phrase in E minor. The parts are inverted, R.H. having a modification of (*b*), and L.H. having (*a*).
9-13	A five bar phrase, extended by falling sequences. Begins in E minor and modulates through D minor to C major. R.H. develops (*b*) and L.H. develops (*a*).
13-16	Overlaps with previous phrase. R.H. as 1-4 but in C major. L.H. Fig. (*c*) grows out of last few

bars of R.H. A third voice part now enters, as a tonic pedal.

17-18   A two bar phrase. New idea (*d*) in all 3 voices. G minor.

19-20   Sequence in D minor.

20-21   Phrases overlap. (*c*) in R.H., (*a*) in L.H. Leads to A minor.

22-26   Overlaps with previous phrase. Returns to tonic key. Five bar phrase extended by sequences. (*a*) in R.H. developed and extended, (*b*) modified in L.H.

26-28   Overlaps with previous phrase. A three bar phrase, forming a short coda. (*a*) developed and imitated over tonic pedal. Ends with 'tierce de Picardie'.

7 Answering Questions on the Music

Sometimes you may be required to answer questions on the work instead of writing an analysis. Look at Fig. 6 and then study the questions and answers given below.

Fig. 6 Ⓐ *Moderato*   Minuet from Sonata in G. Haydn

1st bar of answering phrase omitted, 2nd bar stated 4 times.

3rd bar of answering phrase.   compare bar 9.   Longer extension still.

Perfect Cadence
Feminine ending.

Question 1. Comment on any irregular phrase lengths.

Answer.   (a) 5-14 is a ten-bar phrase in answer to 1-4. Bar 7 is a modified sequence of bar 6, and 9-12 are extended by repetition. (b) 18³-24 is a six-bar phrase, consisting of three two-bar sections. (c) 29-34 is a six-bar phrase, bar 29 being repeated three times at different pitches. (d) 35-42 is an eight-bar phrase, again extended by repetition.

Question 2. Point out one example of each of the following : (a) Alberti bass. (b) Feminine ending. (c) Interrupted cadence.

Answer.   (a) 15-16. (b) 4 (or 14, 24, 34 or 42). (c) 34.

Question 3. Compare 1-14 with 25-34.

Answer.   25-28 is identical with 1-4.

29 corresponds to bar 6 (there being no equivalent to bar 5). This bar is then repeated three times at different pitches.

33 and 34 correspond to 13-14, but 13-14 make a perfect cadence in the dominant key, whereas 33-34 make an interrupted cadence in the tonic.

Question 4. Name the chords in the first four bars.

N

Answer.   Bar 1. Beat 1-2. Tonic triad, root position.
Bar 1. Beat 3.   Tonic triad, first inversion.
Bar 2. Beat 1. Dominant 7th, second inversion.
Bar 2. Beat 2. Dominant 7th, first inversion.
Bar 2. Beat 3. Tonic triad, root position.
Bar 3. Beats 1-3. Supertonic triad, first inversion.
Bar 4. Beats 1-2. Tonic triad, second inversion (cadential ⁶₄).
Bar 4. Beat 3. Dominant 7th, last inversion.

8   Exercises

The student may write out a complete analysis or answer questions on the music or both. The questions are given below the music.

Fig. 7   *Allegro*   Gavotte. Martini

Questions on Fig. 7.
1. In what form is this movement? State the bar number

at which each section begins and the key in which it begins and ends.

2. Name two devices which occur at the beginning of the movement.

3. In what key is the music at the beginning of bars 12, 16, 18 and 32 respectively?

4. Point out one example of each of the following: (a) canonic imitation ; (b) dominant pedal ; (c) tonic pedal ; (d) sequence ; (e) modified sequence.

5. Compare bars 28^3-32^2 with 1-8.

6. Write out the middle voice part in bars 25^1-28^2.

Fig.8 *Vivace*   Two Part Invention No. 3.   Bach

Questions on Fig. 8.

1. Using bar numbers point out the main sections of this piece, stating the key in which each begins and ends.
2. Point out one example of each of the following :—
   (a) imitation ; (b) dominant pedal ; (c) tonic pedal ; (d) syncopation ; (e) anticipation ; (f) canon at the fifth ; (g) sequence ; (h) interrupted cadence.
3. Compare bars 10-12 with 22-24 and 52-54.
4. Quote what you consider to be the two most important themes in this piece.
5. Compare the bass of bars 12-14 and the melody of 24-26 with the opening treble melody.
6. Write out a detailed analysis of bars 12-24.
7. Where do you consider that a return to the opening bars occurs, and what difference do you notice ?
8. Compare bars 46³-54 with 4³-12.
9. Do you consider that this piece has a coda ? If so, where does it begin ?

Fig. 9   Minuet from Sonata in E♭.   Mozart

Questions on Fig. 9.

1. In what form is this movement?

2. Compare bars 22³-32 with 4³-12 and give reasons for the changes.

3. Compare 18³-22 with the first four bars.

4. Point out two six-bar phrases in this movement.

5. Point out two examples of cadence extension in this movement.

6. By reference to beat and bar numbers name all the chords from bars 1-12 (bars 5-8 are one chord).

7. Point out one example of each of the following : (a) a feminine ending ; (b) a cadential $^6_4$ chord ; (c) a dominant pedal ; (d) an inverted perfect cadence.

Fig. 10 *Adagio espressivo*   Adagio. Grazioli

Questions on Fig. 10.

1. Quote the two figures you consider the most important in this piece.
2. Compare bars 13-30 with 1-12.
3. How do you account for the fact that the first part of this piece is twelve bars long ?
4. What leads you to the conclusion that the extract quoted is not a complete movement ?
5. On what previously heard material is bars 23-24 based ?
6. On what previously heard material is bars 21-22 based ?
7. Point out two interrupted cadences, one perfect cadence and one imperfect cadence.
8. Compare bars 17-20 with 5-8.
9. Point out examples of the following :
   (a) a five bar phrase ; (b) a six bar phrase ; (c) phrases overlapping.
10. How frequently do the chords change in this extract ? Name the chords throughout, commenting on any place where the chord rhythm changes.

Fig.11 *Allegro non troppo* Children's Piece. Mendelssohn

Questions on Fig. 11.

1. In what form is this piece?
2. Compare bars 12^3-16^1 with 8^3-12^2.
3. By reference to bar numbers name the keys throughout.
4. By reference to bar numbers point out two tonic pedals, two dominant pedals and one inverted pedal.
5. By reference to bar numbers point out two imperfect cadences, two perfect cadences and one plagal cadence.
6. Is there a coda? If so, where does it start, and on what material is it based?
7. This piece is largely based on one rhythmic figure. By what means is variety obtained?

APPENDIX

WRITING AN ACCOMPANIMENT TO A MELODY

A few paragraphs on the harmonic background to a melody are given on pages 85 and 86, and it is there suggested that melodies written from this stage onwards should be based on a harmonic scheme, or should have an accompaniment.

But a further note on adding accompaniments to a melody is given here, partly because it adds interest to a student's work, and partly because it is being increasingly demanded by Examination Boards.

Whenever a student has composed a good melody he will want to try adding an accompaniment, even though his melody is quite short and simple. But as he begins to write longer melodies containing modulation, a realisation of the harmonic basis becomes essential, even if a complete harmonic accompaniment is not written out.

The following stages are suggested as a course of study. They can be applied at any stage, and to whatever tunes the student is writing.

1. Put in the bass notes at every cadence, stating the key if the tune includes modulation. (See pages 21 to 26, and figure 29 on pages 86 and 87.) Use treble and bass staves.

2. Write out a chord-scheme and then compose a tune above it. Here is an example of a simple melody over a sixteen-bar chord-scheme, assuming a knowledge of modulation:

Minuet

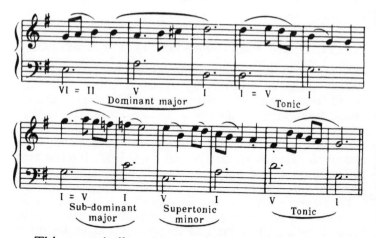

This, or a similar scheme, could be worked several times, using different keys and different rhythms, perhaps in the styles of various dance forms. The melodies would, of course, contain plenty of passing notes and other essential notes, in addition to the chord notes.

3. Add an accompaniment. At first, it may be as simple as this:

4. Then try to get a little more rhythmic variety, and some chord-notes in the right hand:—

Three-part writing is more natural in piano style than is four. Bach usually writes in three parts when he composes a dance in harmonic style in his keyboard suites.

5. Aim at using a few inversions, instead of having all the chords in root position. For example, bars 9 to 12 of the above scheme might go like this:—

6. Experiment with different ways of setting out a chord. This can be done more freely if the tune (perhaps for voice or violin) is on one staff, with an independent piano accompaniment on treble and bass staves. Here are some ways of writing a triad in piano style:—

It is better to adopt two rhythmic figures to accompany a melody, and to ring the changes on them, so that the style does not become too monotonous.

Work out the above chord-scheme, or a similar one of your own, in various keys with the figures suggested above. Then make up other figures, perhaps in $\frac{4}{4}$ or $\frac{6}{8}$ time.

7. Now make up some chord-schemes which vary the rate of chord-change. Examples:—

(a) $\frac{3}{4}$ I – – | VI – – | IV – II | V – – | *etc.*

(b) $\frac{3}{4}$ I – Ib | IV II V | Ib – V | I – – | *etc.*

   Gavotte rhythm

(c) $\frac{4}{4}$ Vb V | I – IIb II | V – Vb V | VI IIb Ic V | I – ‖ *etc.*

Dominant key

Clothe them with melodies, and then add an accompaniment.

8. Vary the texture. A chord in three- or four-part harmony on the strong beats with melody or two-part counterpoint in-between provides a flowing style. Chords can have anything from two to about eight notes, and the number can vary from chord to chord. Beware of having too many notes low down in the left hand. A four-part chord is usually best with three notes in the right hand and one in the left. The bass line played in octaves strengthens the accompaniment, but beware of octaves or fifths between the melody and the bass.

9. Occasionally start by composing the rhythm of the melody. This is particularly helpful if a dance is required. For example, in a gavotte every phrase must start at the half bar, while in a bourrée the phrases will start on the last crotchet of the bar.

10. Lastly, study examples of melody with accompaniment in, for example, Bach's suites or Schubert's songs. Then take one as a model, and write a similar piece, using the same modulations and key-schemes, and the same kind of texture. But choose a different key, and a different style of melody.